THE
NEW YORKER

ENCYCLOPEDIA OF CARTOONS
VOLUME 2

THE
NEW YORKER
ENCYCLOPEDIA OF CARTOONS
VOLUME 2

FOREWORD BY DAVID REMNICK
EDITED BY BOB MANKOFF

Black Dog & Leventhal Publishers
Hachette Book Group
1290 Avenue of the Americas
New York, NY 10104
www.hachettebookgroup.com
www.blackdogandleventhal.com

First Edition: October 2018
Black Dog & Leventhal Publishers is an imprint of Hachette Books,
a division of Hachette Book Group. The Black Dog & Leventhal Publishers
name and logo are trademarks of Hachette Book Group, Inc.

The publisher is not responsible for websites (or their content)
that are not owned by the publisher.

The Hachette Speakers Bureau provides a wide range of authors for speaking events.
To find out more, go to www.HachetteSpeakersBureau.com or call (866) 376-6591.

Book interior design by Eight and a Half, NY, Ltd. 8point5.com

To purchase prints of cartoons, please visit The New Yorker Store,
at https://condenaststore.com/conde-nast-brand/thenewyorker
To license cartoons, visit The Cartoon Bank, a division of Condé Nast,
at www.cartoonbank.com, or contact The Cartoon Bank at
1 World Trade Center, 29th Fl., New York, NY 10007;
phone: 1-800-897-8666; e-mail: image_licensing@condenast.com

The Cartoon Bank® is a registered trademark of Condé Nast,
a division of Advance Magazine Publishers Inc.

Library of Congress Control Number: 2017956541
ISBNs: 978-0-316-43667-0 (hardcover); 978-0-316-43666-3 (deluxe edition); 978-0-316-43665-6 (ebook)
Printed in China
IM
10 9 8 7 6 5 4 3 2 1

"Shall I keep reading?"

LOVER'S LEAP

STEVENSON

JAMES STEVENSON, MAY 19, 1962

LABOR VS. MANAGEMENT
LASSIE
LAUGHTER
LAWYERS
LAZINESS
LET ME THROUGH
LIFE RAFTS
LIGHT BULB IDEAS
LIGHTHOUSES
LION TAMERS
LITTLE ENGINE THAT COULD
LOANS
LOCH NESS MONSTER
LONE RANGER
LOTTERIES
LOVER'S LEAP

"Would you mind putting that request in the form of a memorandum, boys?"

"Then I made the leap from skilled labor to unskilled management."

TOP ALAN DUNN, JULY 11, 1936 BOTTOM LEO CULLUM, SEPTEMBER 3, 2001

"Now, I'm a reasonable fellow, but it seems to me that in case after case and time after time in these labor disputes the fairer, more enlightened position has always been held by management."

"A break every two hours, roast-beef sandwiches, and air-conditioning throughout the negotiations, or no contract."

TOP STAN HUNT, JUNE 7, 1982 BOTTOM WILLIAM HAMILTON, JUNE 10, 1967

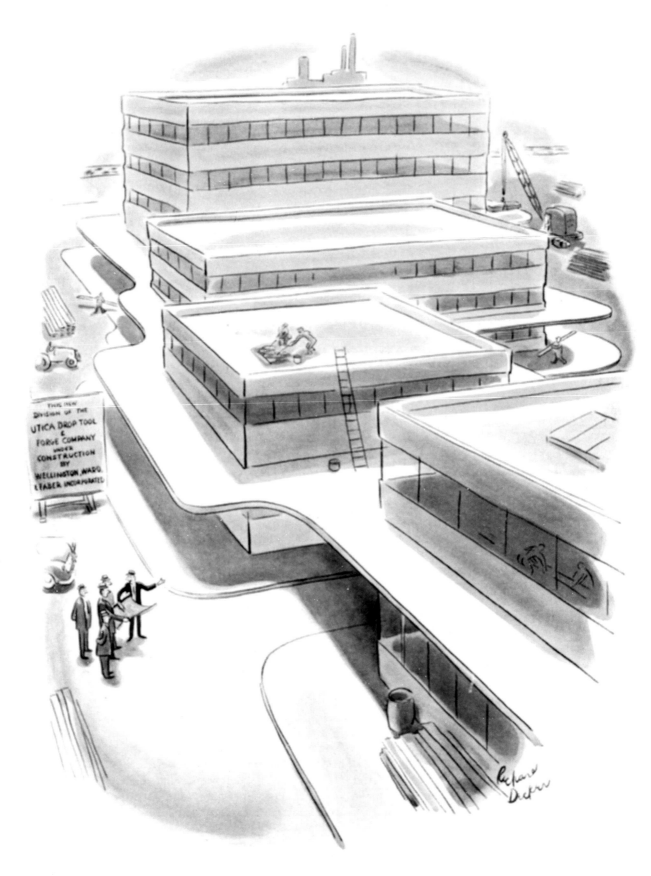

"…and then this functional overhang here will provide
adequate all-weather shelter for picketing."

RICHARD DECKER, JULY 15, 1961

"We also think there should be an escalator clause to meet any cost-of-living increase that may result from the granting of our wage demands."

"You can just say the situation is still fluid."

TOP ALAN DUNN, OCTOBER 27, 1951 BOTTOM WHITNEY DARROW, JR., FEBRUARY 24, 1962

"On your mark, get set, bargain!"

*"...the newspapers, the TV networks, the railroads, farmers, school teachers,
truckers, firemen, policemen—in fact, gentlemen, the whole damn <u>world</u>
is deadlocked on the wage issue. I never thought it would end this way."*

TOP ROBERT DAY, OCTOBER 14, 1961   BOTTOM ALAN DUNN, APRIL 15, 1967

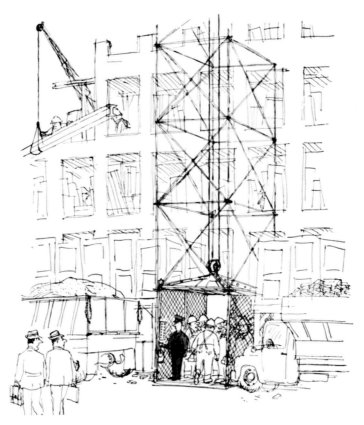

"It's fantastic the demands the unions are making these days."

*"Now that both sides have reached agreement on the basic money issues,
let's see if we can decide who's going to accept the public opprobrium for it."*

TOP EVERETT OPIE, JUNE 3, 1961   BOTTOM ED FISHER, DECEMBER 21, 1981

"What is it, Lassie—is Timmy in trouble?"

"It's out of character. Lassie wouldn't bark right there.
I think she'd be more apt to raise her head suspiciously and sort of whimper."

TOP TOM CHENEY, FEBRUARY 9, 2009   BOTTOM PERRY BARLOW, OCTOBER 25, 1958

"O.K., O.K., here's 'Lassie, Come Home' again! Now are you happy?"

Lassie is merely billed as America's best-loved dog.

TOP JACK ZIEGLER, SEPTEMBER 5, 1988   BOTTOM VICTORIA ROBERTS, AUGUST 22, 1994

*"…and now, folks, listen to that eager bark as Lassie scents her
delicious dinner of healthful, nutritious Vita–Biscuit."*

TOP SAM COBEAN, APRIL 16, 1949   BOTTOM DANNY SHANAHAN, MAY 8, 1989

CROSSED PATHS

Lassie Meets the Hound of the Baskervilles

"Lassie, get tech support."

TOP RONALD SEARLE, DECEMBER 16, 1991 BOTTOM ARNIE LEVIN, SEPTEMBER 10, 2001

"Nothing is funny. We're just having a good laugh."

"If you weren't so funny all the time, I'd probably laugh more often."

TOP GEORGE BOOTH, APRIL 12, 1993 BOTTOM VICTORIA ROBERTS, JANUARY 8, 2001

*SEE ALSO CLOWNS, SMILEY FACE, STANDUP

"You mean all this time you've been laughing at me— not with me?"

"We laugh at the same things."

"We laugh, but it's a mirthless laugh."

TOP TOM CHENEY, NOVEMBER 24, 2008   MIDDLE BERNARD SCHOENBAUM, JANUARY 4, 1988   BOTTOM PAT BYRNES, AUGUST 29, 2011

"Would everyone check to see they have an attorney?
I seem to have ended up with two."

"We would like to request a change of venue to an entirely different legal system."

TOP MICHAEL MASLIN, NOVEMBER 27, 1989 BOTTOM P.C. VEY, AUGUST 18, 2003

"He's sorry, Your Honor, and he's decided to devote himself to making a difference in pigs' lives."

"Well if I can't be a cowboy I'll be a lawyer for cowboys."

TOP MIKE TWOHY, JANUARY 27, 1997   BOTTOM BARBARA SMALLER, MARCH 13, 2000

"Look, I'm not saying it's going to be today. But someday—someday—
you guys will be happy that you've taken along a lawyer."

JACK ZIEGLER, FEBRUARY 2, 1986

TAKE THE PLEA

P EOPLE HAVE BEEN hurling zingers at lawyers since Biblical times. And why not? They're expensive, pompous, and generally perceived as the jackal-headed gods of the underworld. **Lawyer cartoons redress our very legitimate concern that money or bias can tip the scales of justice.** Some of these cartoons remain timeless, such as the Tobey attorney reassuring his client that the longer the jury stays out, the longer he is a free man. Others echo their time, like Barlow's 1954 take on the relatively new inclusion of women on juries. The woman's comment ("I don't listen to the evidence. I like to make up my own mind.") reminds us of the painfully slow march toward justice. Today's cartoons tend to indict the proliferation of lawyers in society, or to confront inequality by asking, "How much justice can you afford?" Flinging these barbs, in a tradition running through Shakespeare, Swift, and Twain, cartoonists remind us that justice is blind. But someone still needs to keep an eye on the suits. ♦

"I'm from Simmersby, Blomm & Tuggarton, down the hall.
Can you spare us a few dense paragraphs of legal boilerplate?"

ED FISHER, APRIL 10, 1995

"My, Grandma, what a big-shot attorney you have."

"Do you think now that we're doing fewer illegal things
we can scale back the legal department?"

TOP DANNY SHANAHAN, OCTOBER 17, 1994   BOTTOM LEO CULLUM, JUNE 30, 2003

"This is sloth—greed is on the top floor."

"Stand erect, feet twelve inches apart. Now bend forward to touch floor between feet—try to keep knees straight."

TOP TOM CHENEY, JULY 29, 2002   BOTTOM BARNEY TOBEY, MAY 27, 1974

"I finally feel I can accept the things I'm too lazy to change."

"Do me a favor, honey, and go get me a latte?"

TOP P.C. VEY, FEBRUARY 23, 2009   BOTTOM JACK ZIEGLER, JANUARY 23, 2006

"Maybe we mate for life because we're lazy."

"That will be the gold standard by which all other naps are judged."

TOP VICTORIA ROBERTS, APRIL 18, 2005   BOTTOM FRANK COTHAM, JULY 10, 2006

"*Miss Roth, send someone in here to roll up our sleeves.*"

"*Instead of worrying so much about your <u>money</u> working harder, why don't <u>you</u> work harder?*"

TOP LEO CULLUM, JUNE 14, 1982   BOTTOM LEE LORENZ, JANUARY 28, 1980

WESTERN YOGA POSES

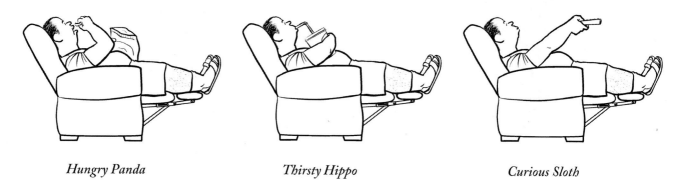

Hungry Panda   *Thirsty Hippo*   *Curious Sloth*

GREGORY

TOP ALEX GREGORY, MARCH 14, 2011   BOTTOM ROBERT WEBER, JANUARY 15, 2007

"When he's awake, he can work circles around me."

"We're operating here on pure adrenaline."

TOP FRANK COTHAM, OCTOBER 9, 2006   BOTTOM FRANK COTHAM, JUNE 2, 2003

"Let me through! I'm a critic."

"Let me through! I'm a businessperson!"

TOP AL ROSS, MAY 13, 1991   BOTTOM WARREN MILLER, AUGUST 13, 1990

"*Let me through. I'm a lawyer.*"

"*Let me through—I'm the victim!*"

TOP HENRY MARTIN, SEPTEMBER 18, 1989   BOTTOM BOB MANKOFF, SEPTEMBER 27, 1993

"Please let me through, gentlemen. I'm a dental hygienist."

"Let me through—I'm morbidly curious!"

TOP DANNY SHANAHAN, DECEMBER 4, 1989   BOTTOM ALEX GREGORY, FEBRUARY 19, 2001

"Please! Let me through. I don't have time to go around."

"Let me through! I'm a quack."

TOP LEO CULLUM, DECEMBER 16, 2002   BOTTOM DANNY SHANAHAN, NOVEMBER 1, 1993

"I know you need a new suit, but first things first!"

*"Now, if you should decide on the term policy, what you save on
the lower premiums could be set aside as savings. On the other hand…"*

TOP AL ROSS, FEBRUARY 12, 1979   BOTTOM PETER PORGES, MAY 13, 1967

"Alternate-side-of-the-street parking has been suspended."

"Damn it, Kimball, don't you know all the words to _any_ song?"

TOP STAN HUNT, MARCH 14, 1964   BOTTOM HENRY MARTIN, JANUARY 27, 1968

FLOATERS

I F YOU WERE STUCK on a life raft, what one item would you like to have? A copy of *The New Yorker* might suffice: you could pass time reading the articles, and, if necessary, it can be used as food. Best of all, you might see a cartoon about your current predicament. While life-raft cartoons bear some situational similarities to desert-island ones, a key difference is the concerns that raftees have about their raft mates—namely, *Will they eat me?* **"Hell is other people"** is never truer than when one is trapped on some inflating plastic with some deflating personalities. (See: Henry Martin's raft occupant, who keeps singing incomplete songs.) But the trope also floats a warmer sentiment: we are, no matter how different or desperate or deserted, all in this together. ♦

JOHN O'BRIEN, JULY 27, 1992

"It's agreed, then. On the movie deal, we hold out for a percentage of the gross, script approval, and Paul Newman and Sidney Poitier in the leads."

"You fellows mind a bit of company?"

TOP DONALD REILLY, OCTOBER 12, 1968 BOTTOM CARL ROSE, AUGUST 12, 1950

*SEE ALSO KAYAKS, MERMAIDS, SHARKS

"What I'm trying to say is we're all in this thing together."

"Look, Joe, I'm calling that wind last night a terrific gale,
and I don't want you crossing me up in your book."

TOP STAN HUNT, JANUARY 23, 1971 BOTTOM WHITNEY DARROW, JR., DECEMBER 5, 1953

TOP VAHAN SHIRVANIAN, FEBRUARY 27, 1971   BOTTOM JOHN JONIK, JANUARY 27, 1992

TOP CHARLES BARSOTTI, JULY 25, 1983   BOTTOM ARIEL MOLVIG, MARCH 23, 2009

"Well, finally!"

ROBERT DAY, DECEMBER 16, 1972

"Where the hell did that come from?"

TOP JAMES STEVENSON, MARCH 20, 1971   BOTTOM ARIEL MOLVIG, SEPTEMBER 17, 2012

"We were doing a nice little business until he came along."

"For Heaven's sake, just because I want to go to the mainland once in a while doesn't mean I'm a social butterfly."

TOP FRITZ WILKINSON, AUGUST 26, 1933   BOTTOM STAN HUNT, DECEMBER 19, 1959

"And pick up a wine—something that goes with fish."

"You're fired!"

TOP JACK ZIEGLER, JANUARY 13, 2003   BOTTOM RICHARD DECKER, JANUARY 23, 1932

"Delivery."

HARRY BLISS, SEPTEMBER 13, 2010

BEDAZZLED

THE LIGHTHOUSE WAS built to be obvious. Yet, as an icon, it is anything but. Virginia Woolf wrote "To the Lighthouse" knowing that its central metaphor could mean different things to different people at different times. Originally designed to steer passing ships to safe harbor, the lighthouse evolved to warn them away from dangerous shoals. The presumption of human presence there suggests a story, but the details remain fogged in mystery. **A lighthouse is isolated but signals community.** Its remoteness makes it exotic; it duties make it impossibly tedious. Latent symbolism, implied backstory, inherent incongruity, emotional charge: What more could you ask for in a cartoon setting? When Harry Bliss's lighthouse keeper utters the word "Delivery" into the phone, it's a light-bulb moment. The impending ordeal flashes vividly in our minds, while the poor soul on the other end of the phone, doomed by taking that order, is still in the dark. Classic. That's why cartoonists have always returned to the lighthouse. It delivers. ♦

"Oh, I don't know. Every night you got to
remember to turn the damn thing on,
every morning you got to remember to turn
the damn thing off, and every six months
you got to remember to change the damn bulb."

"May we?"

TOP JOSEPH MIRACHI, SEPTEMBER 16, 1961 BOTTOM BARNEY TOBEY, SEPTEMBER 2, 1972

"Those darn kids! Ringing people's doorbells
and running away."

"How did you get here?"

TOP WARREN MILLER, JUNE 27, 1964   BOTTOM JOHN O'BRIEN, JANUARY 26, 2004

"If I were only twenty years younger and had my teeth!"

PETER ARNO, APRIL 29, 1961

CLAUDE SMITH, APRIL 6, 1957

"Please, honey, not here."

TOP MISCHA RICHTER, MAY 7, 1955 BOTTOM GAHAN WILSON, APRIL 12, 1999

"And let's remember, children, that the Little Engine That Could was a locomotive of the female gender."

TOP DONALD REILLY, NOVEMBER 9, 1987   BOTTOM DONALD REILLY, DECEMBER 2, 1991

TOP ROZ CHAST, DECEMBER 22, 2003   BOTTOM WARREN MILLER, FEBRUARY 8, 1999

"*What I'd like, basically, is a temporary line of credit just to tide me over the rest of my life.*"

"*Well, thanks anyway for sharing your financial plight with us.*"

TOP J.B. HANDELSMAN, MAY 27, 1985   BOTTOM BOB MANKOFF, JANUARY 25, 1988

"I've heard a lot _about_ money, and now I'd like to try some."

"I'm having an out-of-money experience."

TOP MICK STEVENS, JANUARY 23, 1989 BOTTOM BERNARD SCHOENBAUM, APRIL 22, 1991

"What's the purpose of this loan? Fun."

*"And, hey, don't kill yourself trying to pay it back.
You know our motto—'What the hell, it's only money.'"*

TOP RICHARD CLINE, JANUARY 20, 1997   BOTTOM J.B. HANDELSMAN, SEPTEMBER 22, 1997

"I don't know. I was just in a borrowing mood."

"O.K., folks, let's move along. I'm sure you've all
seen someone qualify for a loan before."

TOP DEAN VIETOR, JANUARY 3, 1977   BOTTOM TOM CHENEY, JUNE 1, 1992

TOP CHARLES ADDAMS, JUNE 28, 1976   BOTTOM LEE LORENZ, JULY 5, 1976

LOCH NESS MONSTER *

*SEE ALSO MOBY DICK, VAMPIRES, ZOMBIES

"If I hadn't seen it, I wouldn't believe it."

TOP LEE LORENZ, JULY 15, 1967   BOTTOM ALAN DUNN, JUNE 11, 1960

"Kemo sabe, I want you to be official greeter at my new casino."

"Tonto doesn't understand me."

TOP BOB MANKOFF, MARCH 28, 1994 BOTTOM EVERETT OPIE, AUGUST 2, 1958

"You realize, of course, that if you take this position you'll be my sidekick?"

TOP JACK ZIEGLER, DECEMBER 7, 1987   BOTTOM ARNIE LEVIN, JUNE 27, 1988

*"You know, you've got something there,
Spikey—the Lone Ranger was a sort of consultant."*

TOP JACK ZIEGLER, DECEMBER 7, 1987   BOTTOM WILLIAM HAMILTON, FEBRUARY 15, 1993

THE LONE RANGER RECEIVES
A DISCONCERTING SMOKE
SIGNAL FROM TONTO...

"Try again, Kemo sabe. This time ease out clutch slowly."

TOP J.C. DUFFY, AUGUST 11, 2003   BOTTOM DANNY SHANAHAN, MAY 14, 1990

"As a potential lottery winner, I totally support tax cuts for the wealthy."

"Professor Roche has just won the coveted New York State Lottery."

TOP DAVID SIPRESS, OCTOBER 4, 2010   BOTTOM ROBERT WEBER, JUNE 26, 1995

"You'll be sorry you made that crack if I win the lottery."

"We'll double our chances of recovery if we buy two lottery tickets."

TOP GEORGE BOOTH, JANUARY 5, 2004 BOTTOM LEO CULLUM, FEBRUARY 6, 2006

"Hit 'em right after they won the lottery."

TOP WILLIAM STEIG, AUGUST 29, 1988   BOTTOM GAHAN WILSON, OCTOBER 2, 2000

"If I won the lottery, I would go on living as I always did."

MISCHA RICHTER, SEPTEMBER 9, 1996

"Hasn't changed much since we chickened out, has it?"

TOP JACK ZIEGLER, AUGUST 25, 1997   BOTTOM CHARLES ADDAMS, OCTOBER 3, 1970

"*Of course, people were much shorter back then.*"

TOP WILLIAM O'BRIAN, MAY 9, 1970   BOTTOM ZACHARY KANIN, JULY 23, 2012

"Goodbye, Lover!"

OTTO SOGLOW, SEPTEMBER 8, 1962

*SEE ALSO AIR TRAVEL, DIVORCE, MARRIAGE COUNSELORS

"*Norman, I don't love you that way.*"

TOP ELDON DEDINI, JUNE 2, 1956   BOTTOM CHARLES ADDAMS, MAY 22, 1948

MAGICIANS
MAMMOTHS
MARRIAGE COUNSELORS
MARRIAGE VOWS
MATERNITY WARD
MAZES
MEDICATIONS
MEDITATION
MEET THE AUTHOR
MEN WORKING
MEN'S CLUB
MERMAIDS
MILITARY MEDALS
MIMES
MOBSTERS
MOBY DICK
MODERN ART
MOSES
MOUNTAIN CLIMBING
MUSES
MUSEUMS

DAVID BLAINE, AGE 60
ONE WEEKEND ON A LUMPY GUEST COT

"Any checks, dear?"

TOP ALEX GREGORY, DECEMBER 22, 2008 BOTTOM BILL WOODMAN, JUNE 18, 1990

MRI Magician

"I got a job!"

TOP PAUL NOTH, AUGUST 13, 2007 BOTTOM SAM GROSS, APRIL 11, 2011

NORELDO, THE MENTAL MARVEL, READS THE MIND
OF HIS CAT, NED.

"Bear with me—I put my hat on upside down."

TOP GAHAN WILSON, AUGUST 27, 1990   BOTTOM ZACHARY KANIN, MAY 4, 2009

"Look, I took my own kidney out."

TOP ROZ CHAST, JANUARY 4, 2010 BOTTOM P.C. VEY, JULY 11, 2011

FOR SUMMER COMFORT...

THE SEERSUCKER MAMMOTH

"Bobby, your mammoth kit is here."

TOP MICHAEL CRAWFORD, JUNE 11, 1990   BOTTOM ZACHARY KANIN, DECEMBER 1, 2008

"Never hunt when you're hungry."

"I think we overordered."

TOP ANTHONY TABER, AUGUST 20, 1979   MIDDLE MIKE TWOHY, NOVEMBER 2, 2009   BOTTOM MIKE TWOHY, APRIL 8, 2002

"I hear they can freeze you until they discover a cure."

"On second thought—you hunt, I'll gather."

TOP PETER STEINER, JANUARY 13, 1992 BOTTOM MICHAEL MASLIN, AUGUST 13, 2007

*SEE ALSO ELEPHANT NEVER FORGETS

"I'm waiting for it to defrost."

"As long as it's woolly I don't ask questions."

TOP ZACHARY KANIN, NOVEMBER 16, 2009   BOTTOM SAM GROSS, MAY 7, 1994

"We're fighting like—well, we're fighting."

*"Maybe you ought to consider making love in the morning—
before you have a chance to piss each other off."*

TOP LEO CULLUM, SEPTEMBER 28, 1992 BOTTOM BOB MANKOFF, DECEMBER 15, 1997

"What's the word I want for that disposition of yours?"

GEORGE PRICE, DECEMBER 6, 1982

"Excuse me for a moment. It's my idiot husband."

J.B. HANDELSMAN, NOVEMBER 15, 2004

*"I should ask, before we begin, whether you're looking
to repair your existing marriage or replace it?"*

"Any healthy relationship requires fundamental acting skills."

TOP MICHAEL MASLIN, APRIL 14, 2003   BOTTOM WILLIAM HAEFELI, MARCH 7, 2011

"Whoa! That's a little clingy."

*"Excuse me, Reverend, but what, exactly,
do you have to do to get a drink around here?"*

TOP CAROLITA JOHNSON, AUGUST 2, 2010   BOTTOM JACK ZIEGLER, JUNE 20, 1994

"I now pronounce you both legally insane."

"Also in all times and in all places to condemn war,
pollution, and non–biodegradable containers, to support the Third World,
and to fight for a better life for the migrant farm worker."

TOP ED ARNO, AUGUST 25, 1997   BOTTOM WILLIAM HAMILTON, AUGUST 19, 1972

"My client doesn't have to answer that."

*"And do you, Rebecca, promise to make love only to Richard,
month after month, year after year, and decade after decade, until one of you is dead?"*

TOP ALEX GREGORY, APRIL 23, 2001   BOTTOM TOM CHENEY, AUGUST 11, 1997

*"Sorry, Elsa, there's just not enough time this morning
for us to repeat our wedding vows."*

"All right, and __now__ will you forever hold your peace?"

TOP MICHAEL MASLIN, DECEMBER 15, 1986   BOTTOM WHITNEY DARROW, JR., JANUARY 30, 1965

"Why, Mr. Larsen! We were about ready to give up on you."

TOP MICHAEL CRAWFORD, MAY 22, 2006   BOTTOM MICK STEVENS, MARCH 15, 2010

"Congratulations, it's a wrnux!"

TOP JAMES STEVENSON, FEBRUARY 25, 1961   BOTTOM SYDNEY HOFF, JUNE 9, 1951

SPECIAL DELIVERY

A LOT HAS CHANGED in the delivery room over the decades. These days, mothers are encouraged to keep their newborns close by, instead of sending them down to the showroom floor to be looked after by nurses. Men—or, in another sign of more accepting times, co-parents of any gender—are expected to be there from start to finish, standing by to dispense ice chips and fight against unnecessary interventions. And nobody would even dream of lighting a cigar.

But new parenthood has always brought with it new conflicts, all ripe for satire; the particulars may change, but the song remains the same. Even a best-case-scenario birth culminates in a terrifying new responsibility—a person! A tiny helpless person that's ours to love and protect, forever! It's such a huge undertaking that if we don't laugh we'll die screaming. But let's all be grateful that, **in these more enlightened times, more is demanded from fathers than showing up to a big glass window with an expectant smile,** floating on a sea of celebratory Martinis. And, really, no one ever should have smoked in a hospital. ♦

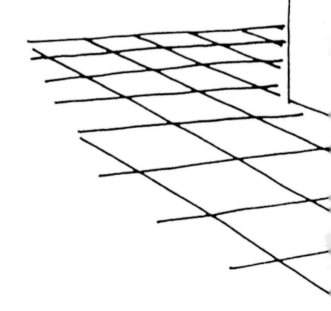

JACK ZIEGLER, DECEMBER 23, 1985

"I've just realized that the nagging little voice inside her head that she'll hear for the rest of her life is mine."

"Same old same old. How about you?"

TOP BARBARA SMALLER, NOVEMBER 22, 1999   BOTTOM PETER STEINER, JUNE 2, 2003

*SEE ALSO DATING, KISSING, SEX

M

*"Thank you for choosing the Lying-In Hospital. As soon as
your parent or guardian has settled your bill, you may leave, and good luck
in recouping your payment from your insurance carrier."*

TOP GAHAN WILSON, SEPTEMBER 8, 2003   BOTTOM HENRY MARTIN, AUGUST 5, 1991

"Well, you don't look like an experimental psychologist to me."

TOP SAM GROSS, NOVEMBER 21, 1994   BOTTOM LEO CULLUM, OCTOBER 31, 2011

"Tough day at the labyrinth?"

TOP WARREN MILLER, JUNE 4, 1984 BOTTOM GAHAN WILSON, APRIL 22, 2002

"We'll take it."

"Actually, I prefer crossword puzzles in the morning."

TOP ROBERT LEIGHTON, OCTOBER 17, 2005   BOTTOM KIM WARP, FEBRUARY 17, 2003

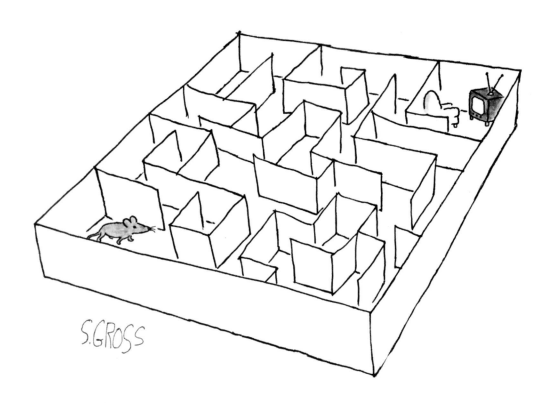

*"Bathroom? Sure, it's just down the hall to the left,
jog right, left, another left, straight past two more lefts, then right,
and it's at the end of the third corridor on your right."*

TOP SAM GROSS, JULY 31, 1978   BOTTOM PAT BYRNES, AUGUST 14, 2000

"Don't forget to take a handful of our complimentary antibiotics on your way out."

"Try this—I just bought a hundred shares."

TOP MICK STEVENS, JANUARY 12, 1998   BOTTOM C. COVERT DARBYSHIRE, JULY 10, 2006

ROZ CHAST, JUNE 8, 1998

"Discouraging data on the antidepressant."

TOP MIKE TWOHY, MARCH 31, 1997 BOTTOM CHRISTOPHER WEYANT, DECEMBER 28, 1998

*SEE ALSO DEPRESSION, *SCIENTISTS IN A LAB*

M

"Before Prozac, she <u>loathed</u> *company."*

"I think the dosage needs adjusting.
I'm not nearly as happy as the people in the ads."

TOP LEE LORENZ, OCTOBER 18, 1993   BOTTOM BARBARA SMALLER, AUGUST 6, 2001

"Well, at least we know she died peacefully."

"Off to meditation?"

TOP GAHAN WILSON, JANUARY 22, 2007   BOTTOM EDWARD KOREN, SEPTEMBER 5, 2011

"Can you be in the moment later?"

"I'm curious, Yogi. Do these students of yours fork over the dough first and then start meditating, or what?"

TOP BRUCE KAPLAN, JANUARY 31, 2011   BOTTOM DONALD REILLY, MARCH 9, 1968

"Showoff."

"Yes, she's here, but in an altered state of awareness."

TOP CHARLES BARSOTTI, OCTOBER 22, 2007   BOTTOM DONALD REILLY, DECEMBER 8, 1975

"For the last time, no, I <u>don't</u> want to hear your private mantra."

"My guru is more tranquil than your guru."

TOP LEE LORENZ, SEPTEMBER 22, 1975   BOTTOM JAMES STEVENSON, MARCH 16, 1968

"I really, really enjoyed your hype."

TOP LIZA DONNELLY, OCTOBER 4, 1999 BOTTOM CHRISTOPHER WEYANT, JUNE 12, 2006

"As long as there's just the two of us, would you mind looking at my book?"

TOP JONNY COHEN, NOVEMBER 7, 2005   BOTTOM LEE LORENZ, SEPTEMBER 10, 2001

PUBLISH OR PERISH

"EVERYONE HAS AT least one good book in them," the saying goes. And many of us dream of unearthing that book and becoming an author. Ah, but not just any author, a *published* author. That would be the life—the glamour, the fame, the book signings! Most of us never pursue the dream this far. Good thing, too, because **meet-the-author events are in fact such dreary affairs.** Authors are reduced to a glorified form of street peddling in the hope of making their book stand out from the thousands of others on the shelves behind them (when the real buyers are online anyway). They sit for hours under a fluorescent glow, watching their towering egos dwindle faster than their stack of unsold and unsigned books, rubbing elbows only with wannabe authors and eBay hustlers instead of the literati they once envisioned. We can all relate to disappointment. But do we really want to read a long, depressing book about it? Luckily, there's another truth to live by: Every author has at least one good cartoon in them. ♦

JACK ZIEGLER, OCTOBER 19, 2009

"Just sign it 'To the Lucky High Bidder.'"

TOP MICK STEVENS, MARCH 24, 1986   BOTTOM DANNY SHANAHAN, OCTOBER 2, 2000

TOP MICK STEVENS, JUNE 24, 1996   BOTTOM CHRISTOPHER WEYANT, APRIL 23, 2012

TOP BOB MANKOFF, JUNE 24, 1991 BOTTOM MORT GERBERG, SEPTEMBER 27, 1982

TOP LEO CULLUM, SEPTEMBER 12, 1988   BOTTOM LEO CULLUM, JUNE 13, 1994

TOP MORT GERBERG, MARCH 17, 1975   MIDDLE DEAN VIETOR, AUGUST 22, 1977   BOTTOM SAM GROSS, AUGUST 26, 1985

ED FISHER, NOVEMBER 8, 1982

*"I can tell you one thing. Being rich beyond one's wildest dreams
doesn't go as far as it once did."*

*"The poor are getting poorer, but with the rich getting
richer it all averages out in the long run."*

TOP J.B. HANDELSMAN, NOVEMBER 26, 1973   BOTTOM JOSEPH MIRACHI, SEPTEMBER 26, 1988

"To wealth, even if it's only on paper."

"Frankly, I hate weekends. They break my momentum."

TOP ARNIE LEVIN, FEBRUARY 10, 1986   BOTTOM DEAN VIETOR, JANUARY 13, 1975

"Would you see to old Peterson? He's in the philodendron again."

"Old Whittington figures if he makes it through March he's good for the rest of the year."

TOP GEORGE BOOTH, JULY 23, 1973   BOTTOM GEORGE BOOTH, FEBRUARY 2, 1976

"Money doesn't trickle down unless there's a damn leak."

"I sold my soul for about a tenth of what the damn things are going for now."

TOP WILLIAM HAMILTON, OCTOBER 13, 1997   BOTTOM WILLIAM HAMILTON, NOVEMBER 18, 1996

"Buzz off!"

TOP BORIS DRUCKER, DECEMBER 26, 1994   BOTTOM DREW DERNAVICH, FEBRUARY 19, 2007

"Do you know a good admiralty lawyer?"

"I have heard the mermaids singing, each to each. I told them to pipe down."

TOP MISCHA RICHTER, MARCH 12, 1960   BOTTOM BRUCE KAPLAN, NOVEMBER 21, 1994

"It's all become so Disneyfied."

TOP JOHN O'BRIEN, JULY 20, 1992   BOTTOM BRUCE KAPLAN, SEPTEMBER 7, 2009

"Oil! We're rich!"

DONALD REILLY, FEBRUARY 28, 1970

"… 'The Guns of Navarone,' 'Von Ryan's Express,' 'The Immortal Sergeant,' 'Rambo: First Blood, Part II,' 'The Bridges at Toko-Ri,' 'Back to Bataan,' 'The Commandos Strike at Dawn'…"

"This one's a bonus for all the others."

TOP JACK ZIEGLER, NOVEMBER 23, 1987   BOTTOM AL ROSS, FEBRUARY 18, 2002

PRICE WAR

"This one's for not asking, and this one's for not telling."

TOP HENRY MARTIN, JULY 10, 1989 BOTTOM CHRISTOPHER WEYANT, JANUARY 24, 2000

"And this one is for being wounded by the media."

"This one is for converting a military base into a crafts center."

TOP DONALD REILLY, MAY 6, 1991   BOTTOM MIKE TWOHY, MARCH 29, 1993

"And this is my pocket."

"This one's for being a nice guy."

TOP BOB MANKOFF, MARCH 14, 1994   BOTTOM ROBERT WEBER, JUNE 21, 1993

Executive Mime

TOP LEE LORENZ, SEPTEMBER 2, 1985   BOTTOM MICK STEVENS, NOVEMBER 17, 1986

THE GOOD TEEN-AGE MIME CHOOSES TO STUDY FOR AN EXAM, WHILE THE BAD ONE CHOOSES TO STEAL HUBCAPS.

THE GREAT WALL OF FRANCE

TOP JACK ZIEGLER, JANUARY 18, 1999   BOTTOM PAUL NOTH, MARCH 31, 2008

Kanin

"The boss says after this you're gonna have to start flossing for yourself."

*"It's pretty simple, Jimmy. We get you some ice cream and then
we throw you off the Verrazano. You got a problem with that?"*

TOP ZACHARY KANIN, MAY 19, 2008 BOTTOM MICHAEL CRAWFORD, NOVEMBER 21, 1994

"I insist."

"Our current medical plan offers a three-day stay for a bullet in the groin or torso,
a two-day stay for a bullet in an extremity, and an overnight for superficial head wounds."

TOP BOB MANKOFF, FEBRUARY 3, 1997   BOTTOM JACK ZIEGLER, JANUARY 6, 1997

"Fixing a leak—and you?"

TOM CHENEY, JULY 24, 2006

"Daddy, can I have a pony killed?"

"Wait—use a knife. It's greener."

TOP MATTHEW DIFFEE, MARCH 21, 2005   MIDDLE DANNY SHANAHAN, OCTOBER 9, 2006   BOTTOM FARLEY KATZ, NOVEMBER 8, 2010

"No, I'm Moby Fred, but I'll be glad to take a message."

"'Moby-Dick'? Again?"

TOP J.B. HANDELSMAN, JUNE 11, 1990   BOTTOM MICK STEVENS, AUGUST 29, 2011

"Have ye seen a whale that matches this swatch?"

"Now you're just being a jerk!"

TOP ARNIE LEVIN, MAY 25, 1998   BOTTOM DAVID BORCHART, JANUARY 24, 2011

"No, we haven't seen The White Whale.
Have you seen Surf Rover or Bunny Hibberd or any of that crowd?"

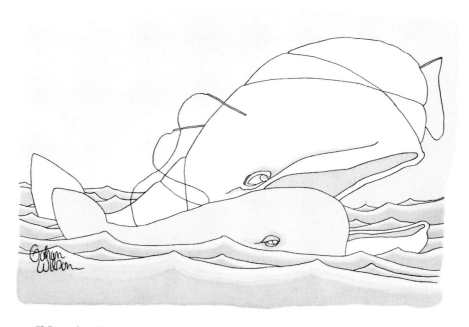

"Now that I've wiped him out, I kind of miss the little peg-legged bastard."

TOP JAMES STEVENSON, SEPTEMBER 30, 1961 BOTTOM GAHAN WILSON, DECEMBER 13, 1999

*SEE ALSO BEACHED WHALES, GOLDFISH BOWLS, ICE FISHING

M

TOP GLEN LE LIEVRE, MARCH 3, 2008   BOTTOM DANNY SHANAHAN, JULY 9, 1990

"*Those old guys really had it!*"

"*I did not say I liked it. I said I didn't mind it.*"

TOP DANA FRADON, JUNE 3, 1967 BOTTOM FRANK MODELL, DECEMBER 4, 1965

"I'm sorry to say it, dear, but I'm afraid I miss my Monet."

"Wow! You mean they got all this in exchange for just one van Gogh?"

TOP JAMES STEVENSON, DECEMBER 14, 1963   BOTTOM MISCHA RICHTER, NOVEMBER 25, 1972

MY KID COULD DO THAT

THE DISTINCTION BETWEEN art and fine art is fine. Especially in modern times. When a painted comic strip by Roy Lichtenstein hangs in MoMA but a printed comic strip by Jack Kirby lines the waste bin, what are cartoonists to think? "Pshaw!" as the *New Yorker* crew would respond roundly from the nineteen-fifties onward. An entire gallery of Picassos fail to impress Barney Tobey's prim matrons: "We've already done this room. I remember that fire extinguisher." The post-representational zeitgeist earns its representative zinger. Now suppose, while Gertrude Stein spins in her grave, that **modern art made itself an easy target.** Magazine cartoonists work on short deadlines and are stylistically stingy by trade. Modern art fell squarely within the cartoonist skill set—Mondrian: need we say more?—and the preponderance of jokes in *The New Yorker* about Pop, conceptual, and abstract expressionism is probably due to this graphic give-and-take as much as to cartoonists' gripes about being taken for granted. Ultimately, from Frank Modell's perspective, the staring contest between canvas and sketchpad ends in a draw. Or as his leery museumgoer mutters, "I did not say I liked it. I said I didn't mind it." ♦

OTTO SOGLOW, JUNE 3, 1961

"We've already done this room. I remember that fire extinguisher."

"I was grinding out barnyards and farmhouses and cows in the meadow,
and then, suddenly, I figured to hell with it."

TOP BARNEY TOBEY, APRIL 11, 1953   BOTTOM JAMES STEVENSON, AUGUST 14, 1971

"*Please! Not at a major breakthrough!*"

MISCHA RICHTER, NOVEMBER 1, 1969

"He'll have abandonment issues."

TOP NICK DOWNES, FEBRUARY 21, 2000   BOTTOM J.B. HANDELSMAN, MAY 7, 1990

"*Mind if I tweak it?*"

"*Of course it's damp underfoot! That strikes me as a
very petty complaint to make at a time like this.*"

TOP BOB MANKOFF, MARCH 22, 2010   BOTTOM LESLIE STARKE, MAY 16, 1977

"Thou shalt not create graven images, Ira. Thou shalt not take the Lord's name in vain. Still looking at you, Ira. Thou shalt keep holy the Sabbath. You getting this, Ira?"

"We've been wandering in the desert for forty years. But he's a man—would he ever ask directions?"

TOP PAUL NOTH, APRIL 18, 2011 BOTTOM PETER STEINER, MAY 17, 1999

"Well, actually, they <u>are</u> written in stone."

MOSES IN CONNECTICUT

TOP HARRY BLISS, MAY 31, 1999 BOTTOM MICK STEVENS, JANUARY 16, 1989

"*Here comes the really hard part!*"

"*I don't mean to dampen your enthusiasm,
but your use of the phrase 'or die trying' is a tad unsettling.*"

TOP GAHAN WILSON, MAY 31, 2010   BOTTOM ALEX GREGORY, AUGUST 23, 1999

"By the way, some of us have begun to feel that
'Because it's there' is not reason enough."

"First you forget the flag!
Now you tell me you don't know how to yodel!"

TOP JAMES STEVENSON, JUNE 29, 1968   BOTTOM MISCHA RICHTER, AUGUST 12, 1967

"Yeah, it's handy, but I still say the old challenge is gone."

JOSEPH MIRACHI, SEPTEMBER 9, 1961

"Seen enough?"

TOP JAMES STEVENSON, JANUARY 28, 1961 BOTTOM HARRY BLISS, MAY 5, 2003

"Hold on. I'm going to have to call for backup."

A Visit from the Procrastination Muse

TOP FRANK MODELL, DECEMBER 22, 1997   BOTTOM KIM WARP, DECEMBER 22, 2014

NEW MUSES

Iphonia	Intoxia	Aerobia
Muse of apps	Muse of flavored Martinis	Muse of fitness crazes

"Poor dear, she's just discovered all these years she's been the muse for a plagiarist."

TOP ROZ CHAST, SEPTEMBER 6, 2010   BOTTOM DANA FRADON, DECEMBER 23, 1961

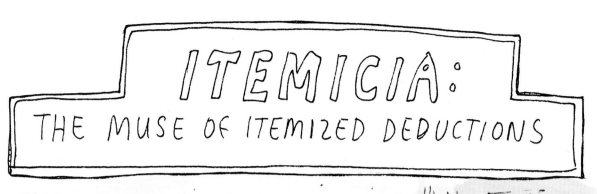

ROZ CHAST, APRIL 22, 2002

"Please be patient with me, Christopher. The arts are an important part of my life!"

TOP SAUL STEINBERG, JULY 29, 1985   BOTTOM EDWARD KOREN, NOVEMBER 29, 1999

"Instead of 'It sucks' you could say, 'It doesn't speak to me.'"

TOP LEO CULLUM, MARCH 11, 1991   BOTTOM MIKE TWOHY, JULY 9, 2001

"Oh, look, I think I see a little bunny."

TOP JASON PATTERSON, JULY 24, 2006   BOTTOM WHITNEY DARROW, JR., SEPTEMBER 14, 1946

"It was a time when men regularly performed great feats of valor but were rarely in touch with their feelings."

"She's not naked, Jake, she's French."

TOP JACK ZIEGLER, JUNE 24, 1991 BOTTOM MICHAEL CRAWFORD, OCTOBER 17, 2005

*SEE ALSO ARTISTS, FAMOUS PAINTERS & PAINTINGS

"How do you know when you're done appreciating?"

TOP JOHN LEAVITT, OCTOBER 17, 2005   BOTTOM JOHN O'BRIEN, MAY 18, 1992

NAPOLEON
NARCISSUS
NATIONAL ANTHEM
NATURE
NEPOTISM
NERDS
NEW YORK CITY
NEW YORK TIMES
NEWTON
NOAH'S ARK
NOVELS
NUCLEAR WEAPONS
NUDISM

"*Where my travel expenses come from is none of your business!*"

"*I was against Russo-Disneyland from the start.*"

TOP FRANK COTHAM, MAY 9, 2005   BOTTOM PAUL NOTH, MAY 24, 2010

"He must have forgotten something."

"Napoleon Bonaparte? Right about there, I'd say."

TOP FRANK COTHAM, JANUARY 6, 2003   BOTTOM CHARLES MARTIN, OCTOBER 13, 1962

*"He's moving his campaign headquarters back to Paris.
He wants to be closer to the French people."*

TOP CHARLES ADDAMS, APRIL 20, 1981   BOTTOM FRANK COTHAM, NOVEMBER 29, 1999

"Let's try one with your hand tucked into your shirt."

"Napoleon was a short man, Stalin is a short man,
Billy Rose is a short man…"

TOP BENJAMIN SCHWARTZ, MAY 20, 2013   BOTTOM WHITNEY DARROW, JR., APRIL 19, 1947

"Is there someone else, Narcissus?"

TOP CHARLES ADDAMS, OCTOBER 21, 1974   BOTTOM DANNY SHANAHAN, MAY 16, 2005

"*I got into the stupidest thing with my reflection this morning.*"

TOP ROBERT WEBER, MAY 7, 1966   BOTTOM BRUCE KAPLAN, FEBRUARY 27, 2006

"Please stand and join us in half-assing your way through our national anthem."

"O.K. with you if I look at it in the dawn's early light?"

TOP MICHAEL SHAW, MAY 12, 2008   BOTTOM GEORGE PRICE, JUNE 2, 1962

"*Can we please sign off just one night without the national anthem?*"

"*The reason I'm singing the national anthem, Steve, is that I'm signing off now.*"

TOP JACK ZIEGLER, MARCH 25, 2002   BOTTOM JACK ZIEGLER, OCTOBER 6, 1997

"Boy, are we glad to see you."

TOP JACK ZIEGLER, SEPTEMBER 25, 2006   BOTTOM JASON PATTERSON, JUNE 19, 2006

"I remember when all this was completely undeveloped."

TOP ERIC LEWIS, SEPTEMBER 5, 2005   BOTTOM MATTHEW DIFFEE, NOVEMBER 28, 2005

"Tell them how hard we've worked to protect their habitat."

EDWARD KOREN, APRIL 24, 2006

*SEE ALSO ENVIRONMENT, GLOBAL WARMING, PARKS

"The fresh mountain air is starting to depress me."

"It's so good to finally get out of the city."

TOP BRUCE KAPLAN, AUGUST 9, 2010   BOTTOM CAROLINE DWORIN, APRIL 16, 2007

"Dad, I've been president of the company for three years, and for three years you've been looking over my shoulder."

"Sure I play hard, but I also inherit hard."

TOP JAMES STEVENSON, FEBRUARY 3, 1968   BOTTOM ALEX GREGORY, MARCH 9, 2009

*"You realize, of course, it's not what you are that counts.
It's who you know. Who do you know?"*

"Gee, Dad, why can't I finalize something once in a while?"

TOP JOSEPH FARRIS, FEBRUARY 13, 1971 BOTTOM LEE LORENZ, MARCH 18, 1961

"When I think how your father struggled to build this business!"

"Luck, son, is when preparation meets nepotism."

TOP WHITNEY DARROW, JR., JANUARY 20, 1968   BOTTOM LEO CULLUM, FEBRUARY 7, 2005

"It's not going to be all roses, son. You'll get a lot of bellyaches about
irreplaceable landmarks and the desecration of our architectural heritage."

"Do you ever stop to think about the nepotism issues I've spared you?"

TOP DONALD REILLY, APRIL 13, 1968   BOTTOM WILLIAM HAMILTON, SEPTEMBER 22, 2003

"When we left off last night, we were on page 15 of the National Intelligence Estimate."

"This is Kevin. Kevin was uncool before uncool was cool."

TOP DAVID SIPRESS, AUGUST 6, 2007   BOTTOM BOB MANKOFF, SEPTEMBER 20, 1999

"*I just figured out why we've never had girlfriends.*"

"*This is Mr. Harrington, our mortgage nerd.*"

TOP MATTHEW DIFFEE, OCTOBER 22, 2007   BOTTOM ROBERT WEBER, APRIL 8, 1996

DORM OF THE DWEEBS

"How's your spring break going, Jerry?"

"I'm a very sensual person. How about you, Mr. Gellerman?"

TOP MICHAEL CRAWFORD, APRIL 5, 2010   BOTTOM STAN HUNT, MAY 10, 1982

*SEE ALSO EINSTEIN, FREUD, NEWTON

"The name's Bond. Duane Bond."

*"You're thinking computer nerd, right?
Actually, I don't know diddly about computers."*

TOP MICHAEL CRAWFORD, SEPTEMBER 25, 2000   BOTTOM LEE LORENZ, JANUARY 22, 1996

TOP JOE DATOR, OCTOBER 26, 2009   BOTTOM LEO CULLUM, MAY 18, 1998

"Pardon me, Officer. Could you direct us to the New York that's illustrated in this brochure?"

TOM CHENEY, JUNE 7, 1993

"A village did raise him. But, of course, it was Greenwich Village."

*"I can't stop thinking about all those available
parking spaces back on West Eighty-fifth Street."*

TOP WARREN MILLER, SEPTEMBER 8, 1997   BOTTOM MICK STEVENS, AUGUST 11, 2003

Shanahan

"It's <u>Brooklyn</u> clam chowder—you got a problem with that?"

MIRACLES ON 34th STREET

Taxi and bus did not collide.

Pay phone worked.

Vender made change without person having to buy something.

Wow! Thanks!

Saw somebody actually put trash into a receptacle.

TOP DANNY SHANAHAN, DECEMBER 18, 1995 BOTTOM ROZ CHAST, DECEMBER 22, 1997

"*Not to blow my own horn, but the ad for my book in the 'Times' called it 'extraordinary.'*"

"*I loved your embarrassing personal essay in the 'Times.'*"

TOP ROBERT WEBER, OCTOBER 6, 1997   BOTTOM BRUCE KAPLAN, NOVEMBER 1, 2010

MICHAEL CRAWFORD, OCTOBER 30, 2000

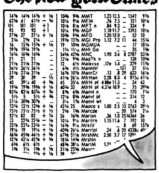
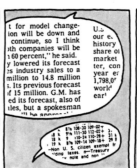

TOP JACK ZIEGLER, JANUARY 3, 1983   MIDDLE DEAN VIETOR, SEPTEMBER 14, 1987   BOTTOM JACK ZIEGLER, SEPTEMBER 18, 1989

"One group gets tiny copies of the 'Times,' the other gets tiny copies of the 'Post.'"

"It's the editorial he was fulminating against when he keeled over and croaked."

TOP MICK STEVENS, MARCH 9, 1998   BOTTOM BOB MANKOFF, APRIL 3, 2000

THREE SCIENTISTS WHO DISCOVERED GRAVITY BEFORE SIR ISAAC NEWTON DID.

"Just what are you trying to prove, Isaac?"

TOP LIANA FINCK, JULY 20, 2015   BOTTOM ROBERT WEBER, DECEMBER 21, 1963

Friends often dropped by and subjected Sir Isaac to a little good-natured ridicule.

J.B. HANDELSMAN, DECEMBER 17, 1990

"Counselor, please advise your client that,
issues of personal safety aside, gravity _is_ the law."

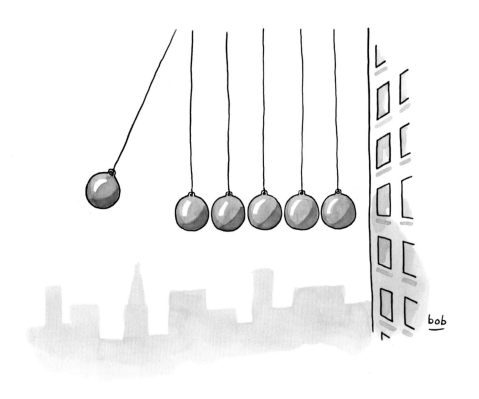

TOP BOB MANKOFF, MARCH 11, 1991   BOTTOM BOB ECKSTEIN, OCTOBER 5, 2009

*SEE ALSO ORANGES VS. APPLES, WILLIAM TELL

Sir Isaac Newton Discovers Gravity. When interviewed, "Newty" said modestly, "I did it for Old England, the wife, and the kiddies."

TOP JACK ZIEGLER, MARCH 7, 1983   BOTTOM REA IRVIN, SEPTEMBER 11, 1926

"You need two more gazelles."

"I know we have to cut costs, but is bringing only one of each a good idea?"

TOP PAT BYRNES, AUGUST 18, 2003   BOTTOM BRUCE KAPLAN, OCTOBER 12, 2009

"We'll feel pretty silly if it's downgraded to a tropical storm."

TOP DANNY SHANAHAN, AUGUST 9, 2010   BOTTOM DAVID SIPRESS, AUGUST 1, 2005

THE NEW YORKER

FELIPE GALINDO, JULY 11, 2011

feggo

PAIRING OFF

I T BEGAN AS A TRICKLE and then became a storm. *New Yorker* cartoons about Noah's Ark appeared infrequently during the magazine's first several decades, but they've since swelled to high tide. While sea levels rise, so, too, does the joke's relevance. One needn't look to the Old Testament for extinction-level events—a peek at today's newspaper will suffice. Noah's plight is eerily familiar and thus ideal for satire. "I know we have to cut costs," says the beleaguered shipwright's wife, as drawn by Bruce Kaplan, "but is bringing only one of each a good idea?" Not to rain on the parade, of course. Besides its pertinence, **Noah's story has everything cartoonists crave: gallows humor, iconic images and, best of all, talking animals.** "You need two more gazelles," the lion informs his crestfallen captain in Pat Byrnes's parody. Call it the carnivore's dilemma. If climate change continues apace, the deluge of flood cartoons will almost certainly turn out to be a mere drop in the bucket. ♦

"When the waters subside, the problem's going to be mold."

"Actually, we're only taking tissue samples."

TOP FRANK COTHAM, NOVEMBER 7, 2005   BOTTOM J.P. RINI, OCTOBER 20, 1997

"Poor thing. The first night out, her husband fell overboard."

TOP ANATOL KOVARSKY, MAY 21, 1955   BOTTOM LEE LORENZ, SEPTEMBER 4, 2006

"I'm tired of people who write first novels."

*"Now close your eyes and go to sleep or
Daddy will read you more of his novel."*

TOP BRUCE KAPLAN, NOVEMBER 2, 1992 BOTTOM DANNY SHANAHAN, DECEMBER 25, 2000

"I feel that I have at least one more unpublished novel in me."

"Great news! Your novel is in a medium-size pile in the middle of the floor
about four feet from the left side of Oprah's assistant's desk."

TOP JACK ZIEGLER, JUNE 21, 1999   BOTTOM DAVID SIPRESS, JUNE 8, 2009

COMING-OF-AGE NOVELS

Claude realizes, once again, that he is flawed.

Mindy sees that she has many issues, almost none of which can be resolved.

Hank gains some insight into things, but it doesn't really matter.

"Kid, we're up to here in bildungsromans."

TOP ROZ CHAST, JUNE 11, 2007   BOTTOM DONALD REILLY, DECEMBER 11, 2000

"The robots have become self-aware and self-loathing.
Now all they do is write novels."

TOP FARLEY KATZ, APRIL 12, 2010   BOTTOM MICK STEVENS, JULY 9, 2001

"Can I nuke something for you?"

"Please, Lady, you're making it very difficult!"

TOP MICK STEVENS, SEPTEMBER 15, 2003   BOTTOM WARREN MILLER, MARCH 24, 1962

"Just think! If it weren't for nuclear fission, we might never have met!"

"I had no idea Howard's arsenal was so big."

TOP CHARLES BARSOTTI, AUGUST 25, 1962   BOTTOM P.C. VEY, AUGUST 28, 2006

"*I certainly hope we have controls before <u>he</u> gets the bomb!*"

PETER ARNO, APRIL 6, 1963

TOP CHARLES ADDAMS, AUGUST 17, 1957   BOTTOM LEE LORENZ, AUGUST 3, 1981

"A copy of the Nudist, please."

"Last night I saw him in a blue serge suit. Zowie!"

TOP CARL ROSE, DECEMBER 9, 1933   BOTTOM WHITNEY DARROW, JR., JUNE 24, 1933

"That's Corcoran. He's revolting against Nudists."

"Excuse me, Ma'am. Have you seen any of Troop B,
Boy Scouts of America, in this vicinity?"

TOP GEORGE PRICE, SEPTEMBER 9, 1933   BOTTOM KEMP STARRETT, JULY 30, 1932

NOTHING TO SEE HERE

T*HE NEW YORKER* was a child of the Jazz Age, and among its youthful indiscretions was a satirical skinny dip into nudism. Naturally, going au naturel is funny, but it was especially so at a time when dinner jackets, fedoras, and ankle-length gowns were the norm. **Against this buttoned-up culture, youth rebelled while cartoonists reveled.** Leading the buck-naked streak was Peter Arno, high priest of louche one-liners. In 1932, he drew a bearded fellow querying a svelte female companion, both in the buff, "Do I wear a black tie tonight for the Throckmortons?" But, by the mid-nineteen-thirties, the theme was wearing thin. Here's Arno again, merely one year later: "A bit boring this weekend. Just the same old faces." Alas, fads go the way of all flesh. Rather than be caught with its pants down, *The New Yorker* quickly swapped its birthday suit for more suitable attire. Nudity still crops up in cartoons on occasion, but mostly to add a frisson to other themes; cartoonists have found other ways to keep their skin in the game. ◆

"See how beautifully your <u>wife</u> has caught the spirit of nudism, Mr. Spencer."

JAMES THURBER, MARCH 11, 1933

"Can you direct me to the Bear Mountain nudist camp?"

"A bit boring this weekend. Just the same old faces."

"Do I wear a black tie tonight for the Throckmortons?"

TOP PETER ARNO, AUGUST 13, 1932   MIDDLE PETER ARNO, SEPTEMBER 2, 1933   BOTTOM PETER ARNO, AUGUST 13, 1932

N

Life Class in a Nudist Colony

REA IRVIN, OCTOBER 7, 1933

JEAN SEMPÉ, OCTOBER 18, 1982

OCEAN LINERS
OCTOPUSES
OFFICE LIFE
OPERATIONS
OPTIMISM VS. PESSIMISM
ORANGES VS. APPLES
ORGAN DONORS
OSTRICHES
OWLS
OXYGEN

"Well, here come the Browns!"

"I love the texture of life aboard ship."

TOP MISCHA RICHTER, SEPTEMBER 11, 1971   BOTTOM PETER STEINER, AUGUST 10, 1981

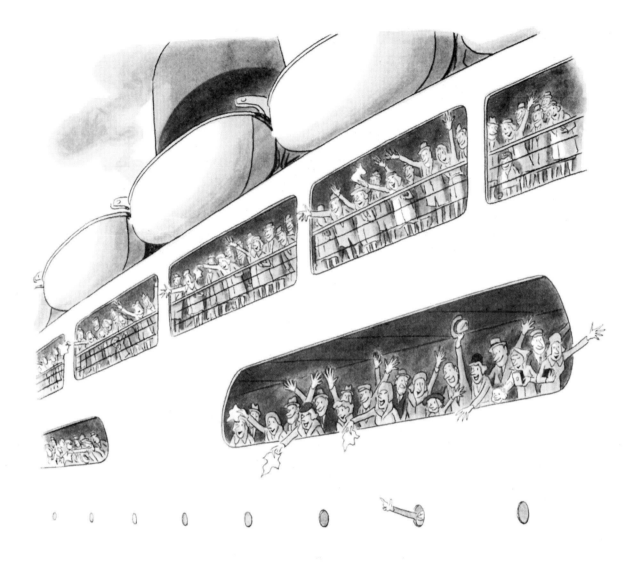

"Everybody's going somewhere except us."

WILLIAM O'BRIAN, MARCH 8, 1969

"Congratulations, Shaeffer! You are now the captain."

JAMES STEVENSON, JANUARY 27, 1962

"Just because you didn't like Europe
doesn't mean it isn't any good."

"Well, it looks as though we've met
our host of new friends."

"Drip-dry, damn it!"

TOP ROBERT WEBER, JANUARY 8, 1966   MIDDLE CHON DAY, MAY 30, 1964   BOTTOM WILLIAM O'BRIAN, SEPTEMBER 17, 1960

"She's lovely, but I don't want to get involved."

TOP SIDNEY HARRIS, AUGUST 2, 1976   BOTTOM FRANK MODELL, AUGUST 29, 1959

*SEE ALSO BEACHED WHALES, LOCH NESS MONSTER, MERMAIDS

"How was it, dear?"

"It fits you like a glove, sir."

TOP PETER ARNO, JULY 20, 1946   BOTTOM EDWARD KOREN, FEBRUARY 3, 1968

"No, Thursday's out. How about never—is never good for you?"

"I don't know how it started, either.
All I know is that it's part of our corporate culture."

TOP BOB MANKOFF, MAY 3, 1993 BOTTOM MICK STEVENS, OCTOBER 3, 1994

"Can anyone remember what our core business is?"

TOP TOM CHENEY, OCTOBER 20, 1997 BOTTOM RICHARD CLINE, NOVEMBER 1, 1999

"Sometimes I think the collaborative process
would work better without you."

"Oh, not bad. The light comes on, I press the bar,
they write me a check. How about you?"

TOP P.C. VEY, MAY 18, 2009   BOTTOM TOM CHENEY, MAY 3, 1993

*"Really, I'm fine. It was just a fleeting sense
of purpose—I'm sure it will pass."*

"Keep up the good work, whatever it is, whoever you are."

TOP TOM CHENEY, FEBRUARY 21, 2000   BOTTOM JAMES STEVENSON, APRIL 25, 1988

*"I try to keep my coffee buzz going
till the Martini buzz kicks in."*

*"You don't get an office.
You get cargo pants."*

*"All work and no play makes
you a valued employee."*

TOP LEO CULLUM, APRIL 22, 2002   MIDDLE LEO CULLUM, AUGUST 17, 1998   BOTTOM LEO CULLUM, APRIL 20, 1998

*"Let's face it: you and this organization
have never been a good fit."*

*"Everybody's getting together after work
to do some more work—you in?"*

TOP MICHAEL MASLIN, DECEMBER 18, 2000   BOTTOM P.C. VEY, DECEMBER 1, 2008

"O.K., now put Tab A into Slot B."

*"Damn it, nurse! I didn't ask for a twenty.
I asked for a ten and two fives."*

"Try jiggling the liver."

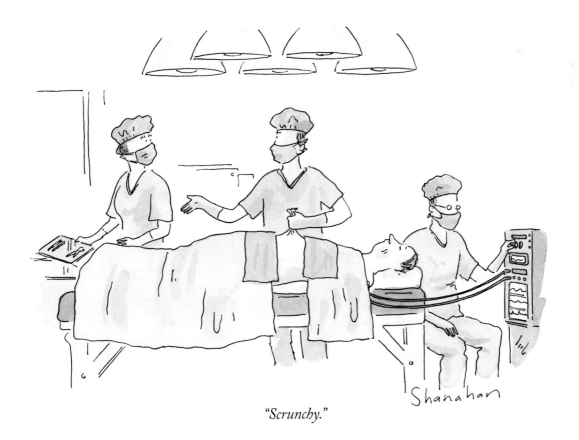

"Scrunchy."

TOP MATTHEW DIFFEE, APRIL 19, 2004   BOTTOM DANNY SHANAHAN, JULY 22, 2002

"Fresh ground pepper?"

PETER STEINER, MARCH 13, 1995

SLICE OF LIFE

LIGHTS, SCALPEL, ACTION! An "On the Air" sign hangs outside the operating room in a 1958 cartoon, highlighting a fascination with medical dramas that began in the nineteen-thirties and continues at full pace even today. A place where a million things can go wrong in a million different ways, with life itself on the line, fascinates us on the screen, but terrifies us in real life. After all those TV seasons of virtual study, most of us still couldn't remove a wart, let alone an appendix. And, we worry, what if the surgeon is just as clueless? That's where **cartoons have proved to be good medicine.** Seeing a doctor suggesting, "Try jiggling the liver," or consulting a set of instructions more appropriate for a paper doll, or crisply demanding, "Spork," only hurts when we don't laugh. By recognizing the absurdity of the situation, we can better swallow the notion that a real doctor has paid more attention to her studies than we have. Or at least knows how to fill out the insurance forms. So ask your doctor if cartoons are right for you. ♦

*"Next, I will use a medium-point roller-ball pen with black ink and,
on the anterior side of the upper-left quadrant, two centimeters below the binding
staple, begin detailing in bold print the patient's previous medication
and treatments relating to present indications for procedure and treatment,
as required on this particular health-insurance form."*

"Next, an example of the very same procedure when done correctly."

TOP TOM CHENEY, JUNE 12, 1995   BOTTOM TOM CHENEY, APRIL 20, 1998

"If I knew where I'd lost the sponge, it wouldn't be lost, now, would it?"

FRANK COTHAM, JUNE 19, 1995

"Half empty, please."

◩ OPTIMIST

◪ PESSIMIST

▩ PRAGMATIST

TOP DONALD REILLY, MARCH 30, 1998   BOTTOM BOB MANKOFF, MARCH 26, 2012

"For Willard, life is a ball. For me, it isn't."

TOP PETER MUELLER, SEPTEMBER 27, 2010   BOTTOM HENRY MARTIN, AUGUST 29, 1983

"Well, whatever you call this, it's irksome. He vacillates between 'Tomorrow is another day' and 'It's later than you think.'"

TOP TOM CHENEY, OCTOBER 10, 2016   BOTTOM EDWARD FRASCINO, SEPTEMBER 1, 1975

*"She always saw the glass as half empty,
while I thought of it as half full. Now I see it as completely empty."*

*"Oh, I don't agree. We have many things to be thankful for.
The natural buoyancy of wood, for example."*

TOP EDWARD KOREN, DECEMBER 25, 1989   BOTTOM ROBERT WEBER, DECEMBER 10, 1966

ROZ CHAST, JANUARY 12, 2004

OPTIMISM VS. PESSIMISM*

*SEE ALSO DEPRESSION, HAPPINESS, INSANITY

"Interestingly, my half of the glass is full."

PESSIMIST:
"HALF EMPTY"

OPTIMIST:
"HALF FULL"

OPTOMETRIST:
"HALF A GLASS
OF WATER"

TOP CHARLES BARSOTTI, JANUARY 9, 2012   MIDDLE MICK STEVENS, JANUARY 10, 2005   BOTTOM ARNIE LEVIN, JUNE 11, 1979

ORANGES VS. APPLES

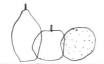

"As an orange, how much experience have you had working with apples?"

"Why don't you try one before you start comparing them to oranges?"

TOP BERNARD SCHOENBAUM, AUGUST 6, 1990   BOTTOM TREVOR HOEY, JANUARY 2, 2012

*SEE ALSO CAT VS. MOUSE, DOGS VS. CATS, GOOD COP, BAD COP

· APPLES and ORANGES ·

EDIBLE
WARM COLOR
ROUND SHAPE
SIMILAR SIZE
CONTAIN SEEDS
GROW ON TREES
GOOD FOR JUICE
NAMES BEGIN WITH VOWEL
SIMILAR PESTICIDE TREATMENT
UNSUITABLE FOR MOST SPORTS

*"I'm sorry, but it just isn't working out between us, Jeffrey.
You're an orange, and I want an apple."*

TOP JOHN JONIK, JULY 15, 1991   BOTTOM EDWARD KOREN, SEPTEMBER 1, 1975

"*Damn it, Ethel, all I'm asking you for is one lousy kidney!*"

"*That liver went to someone who doesn't have such a big yap.*"

TOP AL ROSS, DECEMBER 15, 1997   BOTTOM MIKE TWOHY, JANUARY 20, 1997

"I'm leaving my ankles to science."

"No giblets, but there's an organ-donor card."

TOP VICTORIA ROBERTS, MARCH 31, 1997   BOTTOM DANNY SHANAHAN, NOVEMBER 27, 1995

*"This guy's organ-donor card specifies
'For any deserving conservative.'"*

*"I'm afraid we can't expect much of Holloway.
He left his brain to Johns Hopkins."*

TOP DONALD REILLY, JULY 6, 1992   BOTTOM DANA FRADON, AUGUST 29, 1977

*"If I had waited for the perfect donor,
chances are I'd still be waiting for a head transplant."*

*"And sign here if you'd like to see his organs become
more involved in community theatre."*

TOP MICHAEL CRAWFORD, NOVEMBER 22, 2010   BOTTOM DANNY SHANAHAN, JULY 21, 2008

"And what kind of a world would this be if
everyone decided not to get involved?"

"But darling, we just can't go on meeting like this."

TOP JOHN CORCORAN, NOVEMBER 20, 1971   BOTTOM ERIC ERICSON, SEPTEMBER 8, 1945

TOP WILLIAM STEIG, AUGUST 27, 1966   BOTTOM WARREN MILLER, MAY 23, 1970

GEORGE BOOTH, JULY 25, 1977

LESLIE STARKE, JULY 8, 1961

"*I don't even know when late night begins anymore.*"

"*When I first saw your mother, she was bathed in moonlight.*"

TOP ROBERT LEIGHTON, APRIL 26, 2010   BOTTOM LEO CULLUM, JANUARY 31, 1994

"*If you're so wise, why aren't you rich?*"

"*They're never getting me out in
a pea-green boat with any pussycat.*"

TOP FRANK MODELL, NOVEMBER 23, 1963   BOTTOM MISCHA RICHTER, JANUARY 13, 1968

"And this is an exact re-creation of how an owl would
have looked in the thirteenth century."

EDWARD STEED, NOVEMBER 7, 2016

TALON SHOW

O WLS REPRESENT an interesting set of ideas for the cartoonist. They're thought of as wise, perhaps because of the fact that they look as if they're wearing glasses. They stay up all night. Their appearance is that of a schlubby intellectual uncle—round, soft, and possessed of a genial intelligence—yet they're ruthless hunters. And, of course, there's their signature call: the familiar "whoooo!" that's been a staple of horror moves and pun-crafters for ages.

The combination of these traits proves a rich mine for jokes—about nocturnal activities, about hunting, about wisdom, about that *whoo* sound. There's even ample opportunity to make reference to the Edward Lear classic "The Owl and the Pussy-Cat." And, of course, they're tremendously fun to draw. Those big staring eyes! Those little tufted horn things! That cute little beak! **Always a hoot. ♦**

*"Can you believe that people inhale
the gases we expel —sick, right?"*

*"North face of Everest: howling winds, sub-zero cold,
insufficient oxygen, menswear."*

TOP FARLEY KATZ, MAY 17, 2010   BOTTOM BOB MANKOFF, SEPTEMBER 5, 1988

DANA FRADON, AUGUST 10, 1987

CHARLES ADDAMS, SEPTEMBER 26, 1988

PARKS
PARTIES
PATENT OFFICE
PEACE
PHILOSOPHY
PHOTOGRAPHY
PIANOS
PIRATES
POETRY
POLITICIANS
POLLS
POLLUTION
PRAYERS
PRISONER'S DUNGEON
PSYCHIATRISTS
PYRAMIDS

*"The old persuasive approach is out. From now on,
they put out their campfires or you <u>bite</u> them."*

"When they built this, Jeremy, parks didn't have themes."

TOP DONALD REILLY, SEPTEMBER 13, 1969   BOTTOM LEE LORENZ, JULY 8, 2002

"All I see is more trees."

TOP BARNEY TOBEY, JULY 7, 1980   BOTTOM CHARLES ADDAMS, AUGUST 29, 1988

"This city is going to hell! That used to be a parking lot."

BARNEY TOBEY, DECEMBER 29, 1975

*SEE ALSO ENVIRONMENT, MOUNTAIN CLIMBING, NEW YORK CITY

"Hail to thee, Frederick Law Olmsted!"

TOP BARNEY TOBEY, AUGUST 8, 1983 BOTTOM P.C. VEY, AUGUST 5, 2002

*"The caterers haven't shown up, the musicians are late,
and the elevator is broken. We might as well be living in a Third World country."*

"Remember when everyone used to get drunk at parties?"

TOP ROBERT WEBER, APRIL 26, 1993   BOTTOM W.B. PARK, MAY 9, 1994

*"Hey—what do you say we get out of here
and go back to our own places?"*

TOP MICHAEL MASLIN, FEBRUARY 27, 2012   BOTTOM BRUCE KAPLAN, FEBRUARY 24, 1992

*"Let me guess. You had it up to here with the world of business,
so you packed it all in and started your own winery."*

*"Darling, spotting Todd Mason dressed as a woman—
was that at the Palio in Siena or the Day of the Dead in Oaxaca?"*

TOP WARREN MILLER, JANUARY 11, 1993   BOTTOM WILLIAM HAMILTON, NOVEMBER 15, 1993

MUELLER

"A bunch of friends are coming over to stare at their phones."

"I'd like you two to meet Will and Diane Clampett. Will is the powerful chairman and chief executive office of a large multinational corporation, and Diane is his passive-aggressive wife."

TOP PETER MUELLER, JANUARY 2, 2012 BOTTOM ROBERT WEBER, NOVEMBER 1, 1993

"*They stole all our people!*"

"*I understood each and every word you said
but not the order in which they appeared.*"

TOP WILLIAM HAMILTON, JULY 25, 1977   BOTTOM WILLIAM HAEFELI, AUGUST 2, 1999

"*Honey, you're doing that thing again where you stare into space
and wonder how I talked you into leaving the house.*"

"*You'll have to excuse my wife. She's a bit of a control freak.*"

TOP HARRY BLISS, AUGUST 1, 2011 BOTTOM WARREN MILLER, APRIL 21, 1997

"Quick! Any fire extinguishers?"

"I'm the invention. The inventor should be along any moment now."

TOP FRANK MODELL, OCTOBER 9, 1948   BOTTOM CHARLES ADDAMS, JULY 25, 1988

TOP LEE LORENZ, JUNE 30, 1980 BOTTOM BERNIE WISEMAN, OCTOBER 7, 1950

"Pardon me, sir, are you Mr. Baldwin, the patent attorney?"

CARL ROSE, APRIL 28, 1951

"Death ray, fiddlesticks!
Why, it doesn't even slow them up."

"Damn it, Harlow, aren't you ever going to stop saying,
'Why didn't I think of that'?"

TOP CHARLES ADDAMS, MAY 16, 1953   BOTTOM CHARLES ADDAMS, OCTOBER 27, 1986   BOTTOM WHITNEY DARROW, JR., SEPTEMBER 3, 1949

*"I feel an intense pride, Robert, that I live in a country
rich enough to have war and peace at the same time."*

TOP FRANK MODELL, JUNE 26, 1965   BOTTOM J.B. HANDELSMAN, MARCH 16, 1968

"Now, don't everybody get excited until we've seen the price tag."

"The Middle East peace process seems to be moving right along."

TOP HENRY MARTIN, AUGUST 10, 1968 BOTTOM MICK STEVENS, FEBRUARY 16, 1998

"Could I get a single perfect olive branch?"

"We're presenting this year's award to the tomato—for the way he has deepened our understanding of world-conflict resolution, for fostering the ideals of peace, friendship, and international brotherhood, and for being delicious."

TOP ARNIE LEVIN, APRIL 22, 1991   BOTTOM EDWARD KOREN, DECEMBER 26, 1988

"Someday man will find a peaceful use for my machines."

BILL WOODMAN, JUNE 8, 1987

*"Little do they realize we no longer serve good King Frederick
the Peacemaker but his son, Olav the Homicidal Maniac."*

TOP SIDNEY HARRIS, DECEMBER 28, 1992   BOTTOM J.B. HANDELSMAN, MARCH 4, 1972

"War or peace?"

"Sometimes I think you guys don't want peace."

TOP BERNARD SCHOENBAUM, FEBRUARY 25, 1991   BOTTOM J.B. HANDELSMAN, MARCH 5, 2001

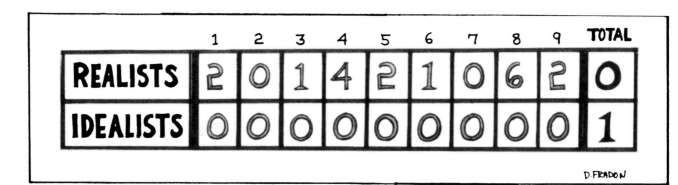

	1	2	3	4	5	6	7	8	9	TOTAL
REALISTS	2	0	1	4	2	1	0	6	2	0
IDEALISTS	0	0	0	0	0	0	0	0	1	1

D. FRADON

"To life, liberty, and the consideration of the concept of happiness."

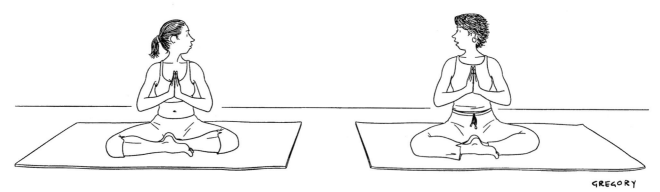

GREGORY

"I just found an Eastern philosophy that's very accepting of S.U.V.s."

TOP DANA FRADON, JUNE 28, 1976   MIDDLE WARREN MILLER, FEBRUARY 25, 1980   BOTTOM ALEX GREGORY, OCTOBER 14, 2002

"I don't think she even <u>begins</u> to grasp Sartre."

TOP HELEN HOKINSON, FEBRUARY 4, 1950   BOTTOM JACK ZIEGLER, AUGUST 12, 1991

ADMISSIONS TEST
FOR THE
DANBURY INSTITUTE OF PHILOSOPHY

1. How many minutes a day do you spend thinking?
   ☐ two or fewer ☐ fifteen ☐ a billion

2. Are your thoughts:
   ☐ like a slow, orderly procession of elephants, or...
   ☐ like rabbits chasing each other in circles, or...
   ☐ like gnats?

3. What are your thoughts mostly about?
   ☐ sex in the year 3000   ☐ parallel parking
   ☐ mealtime   ☐ illness and death
   ☐ getting back at people   ☐ real estate

4. Which outward signs usually accompany your thinking (check any that apply)?
   ☐ wrinkled forehead   ☐ index finger pointing to temple
   ☐ tongue protruding from mouth   ☐ hair standing on end

MAIL COMPLETED FORM TO:

Plato Jones
Suite 410
Danbury Industrial Tower and Rotunda
Danbury, New York

ROZ CHAST, MAY 14, 2001

"Watch out, here it comes again!
'Existence is neither good nor evil. It simply is.'"

"Exactly what is this 'nothing' I've been hearing so much about?"

TOP WARREN MILLER, OCTOBER 27, 1962 BOTTOM DAVID SIPRESS, JULY 31, 2000

MY FIRST CAMERA

TOP SIDNEY HARRIS, NOVEMBER 11, 1991   BOTTOM CHARLES ADDAMS, JANUARY 9, 1978

"Edgar just had his picture taken by Richard Avedon."

TOP JAMES STEVENSON, NOVEMBER 1, 1976   BOTTOM WARREN MILLER, MARCH 25, 1972

"Smile."

ROBERT WEBER, APRIL 30, 1966

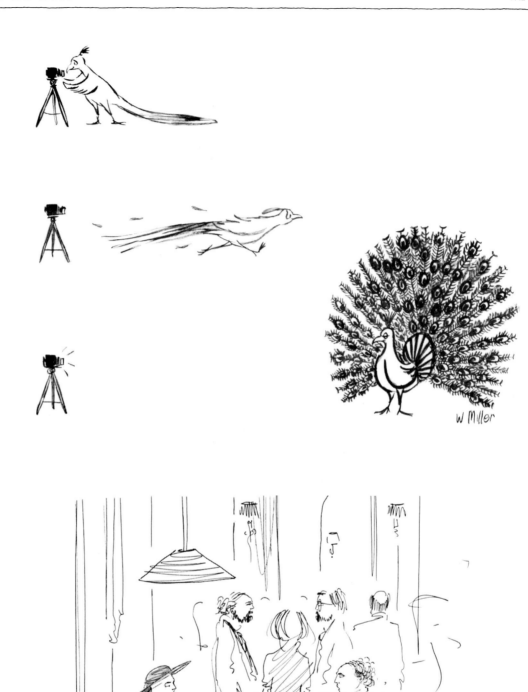

"*Is it you or a Cindy Sherman version of yourself?*"

TOP WARREN MILLER, JANUARY 15, 1979   BOTTOM RICHARD CLINE, MAY 17, 1993

"Got it!"

TOP JEAN SEMPÉ, MAY 19, 1986

*"At the conclusion of this evening's concert, ladies and gentlemen,
I'll thank you for not forgetting the tip jar."*

"Don't make me come down there."

TOP JACK ZIEGLER, MARCH 31, 1997   BOTTOM J.C. DUFFY, MAY 19, 2003

"Personally, I'd have preferred more transit cops."

"And now a whole bunch of rhapsodies by Franz Liszt."

TOP BOB MANKOFF, JULY 21, 1980   BOTTOM MICK STEVENS, JUNE 9, 1980

"No, we're Holsteins. Bösendorfer is a piano."

"It's one of your most inspired compositions, darling,
but I think it bogs down a little in the part that goes,
'They're right-size, they're bite-size, and ever so good for you, too.'"

TOP ED FISHER, MAY 19, 1980   BOTTOM DONALD REILLY, JANUARY 16, 1965

P

"For my next encore, I would like to play another piece written specially for me."

TOP MISCHA RICHTER, OCTOBER 10, 1983   BOTTOM GAHAN WILSON, APRIL 26, 1999

"Not in front of the crew!"

"With the doubloon, you've got the intrinsic value of the metal
plus the numismatic considerations."

TOP GAHAN WILSON, AUGUST 16, 1999   BOTTOM LEO CULLUM, APRIL 21, 2008

"*You* tell him that you find the flag offensive."

"You steered the proper course, Cap'n,
when you had us bury this instead of investing it in the market!"

TOP FRANK COTHAM, JUNE 19, 2000 BOTTOM GAHAN WILSON, OCTOBER 15, 2001

"Pi what squared? Long John, you should be able to get this."

PAT BYRNES, MAY 15, 2000

SWASHBUCKLERS

I S THERE ANYTHING more romantic than the pirate's life? Treasure, adventure on the high seas, naughty sea shantys, hook appendages—all the stuff of legend. The life of the cartoonist is somewhat less glamorous; the only battles he or she is likely to face are against deadlines, ennui, and the odd recalcitrant housecat. But the swagger of the pirate sparks the imagination of the land-lubbing joke-wrangler, who seems to get a kick out of putting the untamable rogue into the confines of genteel situations. *New Yorker* pirate jokes draw much of their humor from the friction generated when you rub the swashbuckler against ideas such as retirement or cocktail conversation. **What, they seem to ask, might a pirate do in the dull scenarios in which we find ourselves every day?** And surely this must speak to the desire, held by respectable folks and ink-stained wretches alike, to slip the bonds of polite society and run off to sea. A cartoonist can dream, can't he? Or at the very least, get a pet parrot. ♦

P. BYRNES.

"*Who ordered the bravest tuna on all the seven seas,
anointed with the spice of faraway lands, on wheat toast?*"

"*The eye patch is just to keep me from fixating on the hook.*"

TOP JOE DATOR, JANUARY 8, 2007 BOTTOM ERIC LEWIS, MARCH 19, 2007

*SEE ALSO DESERT ISLAND, OCEAN LINERS

P

"Jazzercise, Lido deck, 4 P.M."

"You'd be amazed how quickly a boat like that pays for itself."

TOP NICK DOWNES, SEPTEMBER 27, 2004   BOTTOM DAVID BORCHART, JUNE 1, 2009

"*We'd like to take a majority position in your poetry.*"

TOP DAVID PASCAL, JUNE 5, 1989   BOTTOM EDWARD KOREN, MARCH 15, 2010

*"It's National Poetry Month, Marion,
and by God we're gonna read some poetry."*

TOP JOHN O'BRIEN, OCTOBER 22, 2001 BOTTOM DAVID SIPRESS, APRIL 17, 2000

POETS' CORNER

With the aid of an abacus,
Elizabeth Barret Browing counts the ways.

T.S. Eliot lacks
the courage to eat a peach.

Keat's heart aches, and a drowsy
numbness pains his sense.

Walt Whitman sounds his barbaric yawp
over the roofs of the world.

J.B. HANDELSMAN, APRIL 1, 1991

*SEE ALSO MEET THE AUTHOR, UNEMPLOYMENT, WRITERS

P

"*Catherine's gift to us tonight is her poetry.*"

TOP EDWARD KOREN, FEBRUARY 10, 1992 BOTTOM JACK ZIEGLER, APRIL 4, 2005

"Do your owners treat you well? Mine are very kind."

"What I want is an address that speaks with one voice."

TOP J.B. HANDELSMAN, DECEMBER 20, 1999   BOTTOM BERNARD SCHOENBAUM, FEBRUARY 17, 1992

"Listen, pal! I didn't spend seven million bucks to
get here so I could yield the floor to you."

"I'm not spinning—I'm contextualizing."

TOP DANA FRADON, JANUARY 12, 1987   BOTTOM BARBARA SMALLER, NOVEMBER 25, 2002

"I'd like to stall this project into the ground—
hand it over to one of our action committees."

"With the Suzuki method,
they start them campaigning as
early as three or four."

"We used to feel your pain,
but that's no longer our policy."

TOP TOM CHENEY, JUNE 1, 1998   MIDDLE MIKE TWOHY, MARCH 9, 1998   BOTTOM MICK STEVENS, NOVEMBER 20, 1995

"You can't legislate morality, thank heaven."

JOSEPH FARRIS, FEBRUARY 14, 1977

"Wait, those weren't lies. That was spin!"

"Let me be vague."

TOP MORT GERBERG, APRIL 20, 1998   BOTTOM DAVID SIPRESS, DECEMBER 1, 2003

"Congratulations, Dave! I don't think I've read a more beautifully evasive and subtly misleading public statement in all my years in government."

TOP ED ARNO, JULY 20, 1992   BOTTOM JAMES STEVENSON, JUNE 15, 1987

*"This is the New York 'Times' Business Poll again, Mr. Landau.
Do you feel better or worse about the economy than you did twenty minutes ago?"*

"One final question: Do you now own or have you ever owned a fur coat?"

TOP J.B. HANDELSMAN, JUNE 7, 1993   BOTTOM MICK STEVENS, APRIL 3, 1989

"I'm undecided, but that doesn't mean I'm apathetic or uninformed."

"That's the worst set of opinions I've heard in my entire life."

TOP CHARLES BARSOTTI, JUNE 16, 1980   BOTTOM ROBERT WEBER, NOVEMBER 24, 1975

"A final question. Would you put your money where your mouth is?"

"No, I don't want to know what my approval rating is."

TOP WHITNEY DARROW, JR., JULY 14, 1975   BOTTOM DANA FRADON, SEPTEMBER 25, 2000

*SEE ALSO ELECTIONS, ETHICS, GOVERNMENT

"What I drink and what I tell the pollsters I drink are two different things."

"The latest poll shows your approval rating holding steady at a hundred per cent."

TOP LEO CULLUM, SEPTEMBER 11, 2006   BOTTOM LEE LORENZ, MAY 29, 2006

"We're lucky. This stream could be next to a paper mill instead of a brewery."

"Where there's smoke, there's money."

TOP VAHAN SHIRVANIAN, MAY 16, 1970   BOTTOM JOSEPH MIRACHI, APRIL 1, 1985

"It's great! You just tell him how much pollution your company is responsible
for and he tells you how many trees you have to plant to atone for it."

ED FISHER, OCTOBER 16, 1989

"Wasn't this blue back in 1947?"

"I, too, want to preserve the environment, just as it is: acid rain,
holes in the ozone layer, lots of crap in the air."

TOP LEE LORENZ, JULY 12, 2010   BOTTOM J.B. HANDELSMAN, OCTOBER 18, 1999

"I just invented fire and pollution."

TOP JOSEPH FARRIS, MARCH 14, 1970   BOTTOM BRUCE KAPLAN, JANUARY 17, 2000

"Please, Lord, enough already."

*"Under the Freedom of Information Act,
I'm requesting that you disclose what you have on me in your files."*

TOP ARNIE LEVIN, DECEMBER 27, 1993 BOTTOM DANA FRADON, OCTOBER 25, 1993

*"Anyway, we'd love to have
You on board for the Creighton deal."*

*"2br, 1.5ba, PreWr, hwd fl., EIK, hi ceil.,
lg. clsts, 24 hr. drmn, riv. vu, 800K."*

TOP MIKE TWOHY, JUNE 3, 1994   BOTTOM JOSE ARROYO, APRIL 21, 2008

"And may we continue to be worthy of consuming a
disproportionate share of this planet's resources."

TOP J.B. HANDELSMAN, MARCH 29, 1999   BOTTOM LEE LORENZ, JULY 20, 1992

ACCESS DENIED

"Actually, it's pronounced 'An-hel.'"

TOP DANA FRADON, SEPTEMBER 23, 2002   BOTTOM LEO CULLUM, AUGUST 24, 2009

"Surely it can't be twenty-five years already!"

"The truth serum made you say some very hurtful things."

TOP GAHAN WILSON, MARCH 26, 2001   BOTTOM FRANK COTHAM, AUGUST 4, 2003

"*Apparently, nobody up there gives a crap
that daylight-saving time is over.*"

"*Sometimes it seems there just aren't enough hours in the day.*"

TOP JACK ZIEGLER, NOVEMBER 8, 2004 BOTTOM MICHAEL CRAWFORD, SEPTEMBER 5, 2016

Victoria Roberts R.

"You're born, you deconstruct your childhood, and then you die."

"You've got to _want_ to connect the dots, Mr. Michaelson."

TOP VICTORIA ROBERTS, DECEMBER 7, 1998   BOTTOM DANNY SHANAHAN, OCTOBER 8, 2001

"*Would it be possible to speak with the personality that pays the bills?*"

"*Woulda, coulda, shoulda. Next!*"

TOP LEO CULLUM, APRIL 9, 2001 BOTTOM BRUCE KAPLAN, JANUARY 9, 1995

"Why do you think you cross the road?"

"Don't worry. Fantasies about devouring the doctor are perfectly normal"

TOP ARNIE LEVIN, NOVEMBER 12, 1990   BOTTOM LEE LORENZ, FEBRUARY 4, 1991

"*There are no wrong answers—*
only perceived threats to national security."

"*Can you give me some sort of metaphor for how you're feeling?*"

TOP MIKE TWOHY, APRIL 23, 2007   BOTTOM SHANNON WHEELER, JANUARY 13, 2014

COUCH CASTING

I N ALL HIS voluminous writings, Freud never mentioned the gag cartoon. What could account for this? Repression? Denial? Maybe. More likely, he realized that sometimes a cartoon is just a cartoon. **Freud may have ignored the gag cartoon, but the gag cartoon did not ignore Freud.** As early as the nineteen-thirties, artists such as Whitney Darrow, Jr., peopled their cartoons with analysts straight out of Vienna Central Casting. Two decades later, William Steig was still using the same agency. The obsession with the analytical situation continues to this day. In the past five years, the magazine has run more than forty cartoons depicting the shrink and the shrunk,

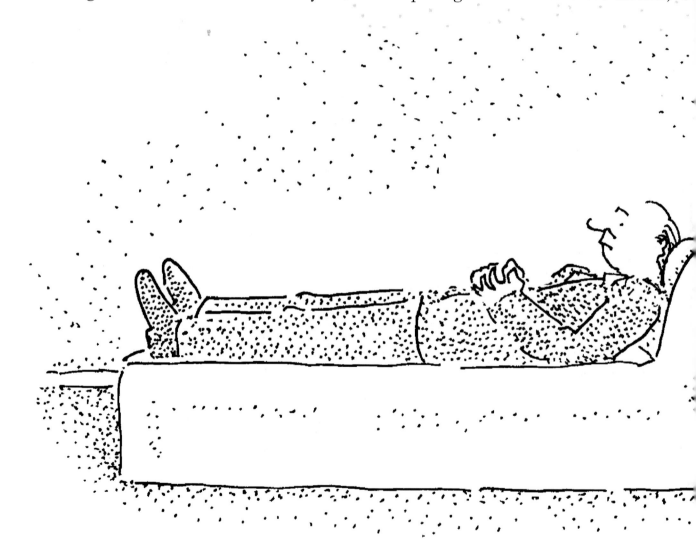

the practitioner and the practiced-upon. And, of course, the couch. As in a dream, the components of the situation have become peculiarly malleable. The analyst may be a rabbit and the analysand may be a chicken or even a bowling pin. And the couch may be reconfigured as an ejection seat. In a Lee Lorenz cartoon, human beings have departed the scene entirely, and the psychiatrist's office is inside a mousehole. What are the cartoonists saying to us and about us? Well, let's just say that to find out we have a lot of work to do together—an awful lot. But now, at least, maybe vee can begin. Actually, not now, because our time is up. ♦

"Look, you're not the only one with problems."

BOB MANKOFF, JULY 21, 2008

"You think I turn a profit on the actual therapy?"

"They moved my bowl."

TOP DREW DERNAVICH, APRIL 11, 2016   MIDDLE DONALD REILLY, JUNE 10, 1991   BOTTOM CHARLES BARSOTTI, JULY 17, 1995

TOP ROZ CHAST, AUGUST 27, 2012   BOTTOM TOM TORO, APRIL 2, 2012

"Just so you know, I'm taking all this with me into the afterlife."

"On the whole, they're much as I visualized them."

TOP FRANK COTHAM, DECEMBER 6, 2010   BOTTOM SMILBY, AUGUST 21, 1965

"This could be the discovery of the century.
Depending, of course, on how far down it goes."

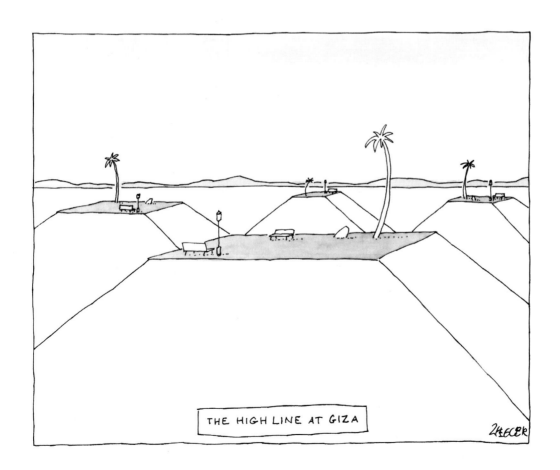

TOP WILLIAM O'BRIAN, JULY 19, 1958 BOTTOM JACK ZIEGLER, FEBRUARY 11, 2013

"I think I've spotted your problem."

"Sorry, Akhet, but we've decided to stick with pyramids."

TOP GAHAN WILSON, JANUARY 11, 2010   BOTTOM FRANK MODELL, FEBRUARY 29, 1988

"Yeah, but the one in Vegas has an endless shrimp buffet."

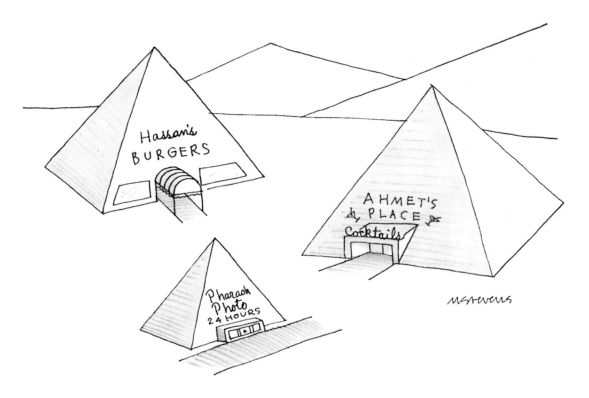

The Lesser Pyramids

TOP MATTHEW DIFFEE, OCTOBER 15, 2007   BOTTOM MICK STEVENS, OCTOBER 10, 1988

SAUL STEINBERG, JULY 29, 1961

QUARRELS
QUESTION MARKS
QUESTIONS
QUICKSAND
QUIZ SHOW
QUOTATIONS

"I'm late, you're angry—we quarrel."

*"No, Charles, I don't have a cold.
What you hear in my voice is contempt."*

TOP MICHAEL MASLIN, NOVEMBER 6, 1978   BOTTOM WILLIAM HAMILTON, MARCH 22, 1976

*"How many times do I have to tell you, Jocelyn,
'I won't dance! Why should I? I won't dance!
How could I? I won't dance! Merci beaucoup!'"*

*"That's not looking unpleasant.
<u>This</u> is looking unpleasant."*

TOP JACK ZIEGLER, JANUARY 19, 1976   BOTTOM DEAN VIETOR, MAY 24, 1976

"I admitted I was wrong. Right?"

WHITNEY DARROW, JR., JANUARY 16, 1960

"First, can we agree that it's a big back yard?"

"You ruined the best two hundred years of my life.
I hope you're satisfied."

TOP CHARLES BARSOTTI, JULY 29, 2002 BOTTOM LEE LORENZ, APRIL 14, 1975 BOTTOM OTTO SOGLOW, OCTOBER 14, 1944

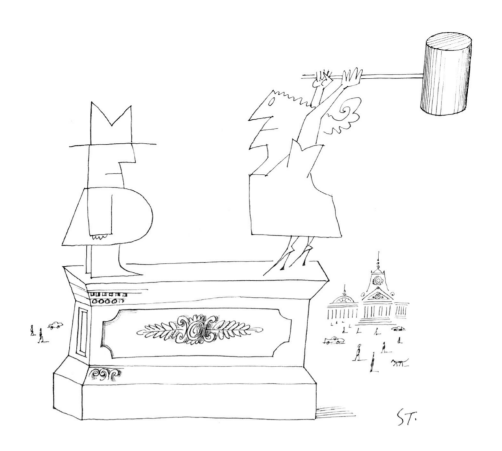

"Dauphin! Stop teasing La Infanta!"

TOP SAUL STEINBERG, OCTOBER 21, 1961   BOTTOM PETER PORGES, NOVEMBER 16, 1987

*SEE ALSO DIVORCE, FAMILY, MARRIAGE COUNSELORS

*"Before I answer that, is this or is this not going to be
part of your goddamn novel?"*

"Give me a for instance."

TOP LEE LORENZ, MAY 17, 1976   BOTTOM EDWARD KOREN, FEBRUARY 23, 1976

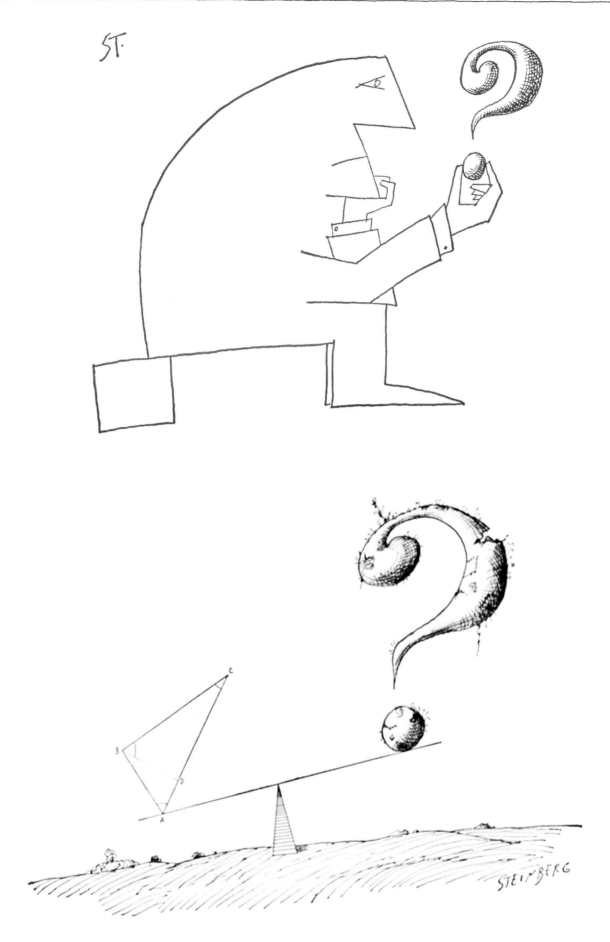

TOP SAUL STEINBERG, SEPTEMBER 24, 1960   BOTTOM SAUL STEINBERG, JULY 23, 1960

TOP SAM GROSS, JUNE 2, 1973   BOTTOM SAUL STEINBERG, JANUARY 30, 1965

"I still don't have all the answers, but I'm beginning to ask the right questions."

"If I may, Mr. Perlmutter, I'd like to answer your question with a question."

TOP LEE LORENZ, FEBRUARY 27, 1989   BOTTOM MICHAEL MASLIN, FEBRUARY 22, 1988

"Special Agent Vickers and I have a few questions for you, Ericson."

"We'd now like to open the floor to shorter speeches disguised as questions."

TOP DANNY SHANAHAN, MARCH 19, 2001 BOTTOM STEVE MACONE, OCTOBER 18, 2010

The Big Questions

"Where are we going?"
"Where do we come from?"

"Why?"

"When do we eat?"

"Where are the men?"

"But is it Art?"

"Are we there yet?"

HUGUETTE MARTEL, APRIL 8, 1991

"*I have just one more question—will it make me happy?*"

DAVID SIPRESS, MAY 31, 2010

"Quicksand in a modern office building? Don't be silly."

"In New York, we wouldn't call this quick."

TOP CHARLES BARSOTTI, DECEMBER 5, 2005   BOTTOM LIAM WALSH, MAY 18, 2015

"Thank God for the elephant."

"Some parts of quicksand are quicker than other parts, apparently."

"Quicksand or not, Barclay, I've half a mind to struggle."

TOP PETER KUPER, SEPTEMBER 12, 2016   MIDDLE JAMES STEVENSON, JUNE 4, 1960   BOTTOM RICHARD TAYLOR, AUGUST 29, 1942

WAIST DEEP

QUICKSAND TENDS TO rank high on childhood's long and elaborate list of fears. What a particularly horrifying and gruesome way to die, sucked down into the hungry maw of the earth itself! Despite the term, death by quicksand seemed like a grotesquely attenuated process—so much time to flail, to suffer, to think about where you'd gone wrong in life. Time enough, as cartoons show us, to get in one last quip.

As adults, we come to realize that our fear of quicksand was unfounded. We never actually run into it. In fact, we start to wonder whether quicksand is even real, or just one of those menaces—like the Blob and Freddy Krueger—that screenwriters have conjured for their convenience. As it happens, quicksand does exist, but, experts tell us, it's impossible for a human to sink any farther than the waist. No maw awaits. **Survival is assured—so long as we don't panic.** And how hard can that be? It's only quicksand. Only quicksand. Only quicksand. ♦

*SEE ALSO DOOMSAYERS, SANDBOXES, VOLCANOS

"Top drawer, that chap. Who else would think of waving goodbye?"

JAMES STEVENSON, NOVEMBER 19, 1960

"'No Brainers' for a thousand, Alex."

"You're absolutely right, sir. And now that you've won a free trip to Chile, would you care to try for return passage?"

TOP BOB MANKOFF, SEPTEMBER 5, 1994   BOTTOM JAMES MULLIGAN, APRIL 19, 1952

"*I must say the occasion is somewhat dampened by that clobbering we took on 'College Bowl.'*"

ROBERT DAY, JUNE 3, 1967

"You're *right*, sir! Washington *is* the capital of the United States.
Now for the sixty-five-thousand-three-hundred-and-thirty-six-dollar jackpot question.
Tell us, Mr. Potter, what is the population of Shekar Dzong, Tibet?"

TOP CHARLES MARTIN, MARCH 25, 1950 BOTTOM J.B. HANDELSMAN, MARCH 30, 1992

"You can't tell. He may have won a bundle on a quiz show."

"You'd be sunk unless they had a category like 'Bar-and-Grills.'"

TOP WHITNEY DARROW, JR., AUGUST 25, 1956   BOTTOM JOSEPH MIRACHI, DECEMBER 3, 1955

"This happy breed of men, this little world, this blessed plot,
this earth, this realm, this east end of Long Island!"

TOP CHARLES BARSOTTI, FEBRUARY 20, 1989   BOTTOM J.B. HANDELSMAN, JULY 23, 1990

*"Well, the lowing herd winds slowly o'er the lea.
Time to break out the old Martinis, I guess."*

TOP STAN HUNT, NOVEMBER 21, 1964 BOTTOM MICK STEVENS, JULY 30, 1990

SAY AGAIN?

I N THE QUOTATION GAG, stored cultural knowledge is exchanged for a laugh. You read the quote. Instantly, the question flashes across your brain: *Where did I hear that?* Thereby triggering a tiny little mental Rolodex to flip and flip, until the match clicks into place. See, you did learn something in college.

And, of course, it's not quite an exact match. Which is part of the satisfaction: you read the quote, shining with its nimbus of cultural context, and you see, too, immediately, what's been changed in the quote or how the quote has been changed by the drawing it's attached to. Thereby **giving you a sense of ownership, as if somehow it were your joke,** too. Some

BARTLETT'S UNFAMILIAR QUOTATIONS

"Never wear white after Labor Day."
— Plato

"Once the transmission goes, the whole car goes."
— William Shakespeare

"It's better to own than to rent."
— Sigmund Freud

ROZ CHAST, FEBRUARY 19, 1990

readers (and we're not saying you're one of them) react with a smug pat on their own college-educated backs, happy that they know who Horace Greeley was, or, anyway, what he said.

That's the quotation gag. And then artists like Roz Chast take it further. She double-backs on the élitist qualities of the trope by making fun of the entire idea of citing quotations. We can only conclude with a quote (of course) from Roz herself, who once said, "Even if you don't have any dishes, you need a celery dish." And if that makes sense to you, we've got a lovely nickel-plated statuette for you, of Horace Greeley. And yes, he's pointing westward. ♦

Bartlett's Expanded Quotations

"Sally is the pretty one, June is the smart one."
~May Lipton

"I could have bought an entire brownstone for $12,000 in those days."
—Ralph Sims

"So you think the world owes you a living, is that right?"
—Mr. and Mrs. Edgewater

ROZ CHAST, FEBRUARY 4, 1991

"No man is an island, entire of itself; every man is a piece of the continent,
a part of the main; if a clod be washed away by the sea, Europe is the less, as well
as if a promontory were, as well as if a manor of thy friends or of thine own were;
any man's death diminishes me, because I am involved in mankind;
and therefore never send to know for whom the bell tolls; it tolls for thee."

"Friend, you sure said a mouthful!"

ELDON DEDINI, MAY 26, 1973

"As the days dwindle down to a precious few,
why shouldn't you order what you want?"

"Now, remember, dear.
Speak softly and carry a big stick."

"Oops! I must go down to the seas again."

TOP FRANK MODELL, NOVEMBER 20, 1965   MIDDLE WHITNEY DARROW, JR., FEBRUARY 3, 1962   BOTTOM ROBERT WEBER, MAY 25, 1968

JACK ZIEGLER, MAY 31, 1999

RAINBOWS
RAPUNZEL
REAL ESTATE
RED
RELIGION
RENAISSANCE
REPORT CARDS
RESTAURANTS
ROBIN HOOD
ROBOTS
ROCK 'N' ROLL
ROYALTY
RUBIK'S CUBE

"Why, these are nothing but a lot of tax-and-spend proposals!"

"I hear he's really loaded."

TOP DONALD REILLY, NOVEMBER 9, 1998   BOTTOM MISCHA RICHTER, SEPTEMBER 3, 1955

YVES SAINT LAURENT
FINDS A POT OF GOLD LAMÉ
AT THE END OF THE RAINBOW.

TOP MICHAEL MASLIN, NOVEMBER 7, 1994   BOTTOM CHARLES ADDAMS, DECEMBER 4, 1954

EDWARD KOREN, OCTOBER 2, 1971

*"One of the reasons I married Buffleton was
that he was always chasing rainbows."*

R

"But what if it's at the other end?"

TOP STAN HUNT, AUGUST 16, 1982 BOTTOM OTTO SOGLOW, JULY 8, 1961

RAPUNZEL IN THE MORNING

RAPUNZEL AT THE HOP

TOP ALEX GREGORY, MAY 23, 2005   BOTTOM DANNY SHANAHAN, APRIL 2, 1990

"What say you just buzz me in tonight, honey?"

TOP ROZ CHAST, MAY 19, 2003   BOTTOM JACK ZIEGLER, AUGUST 8, 2011

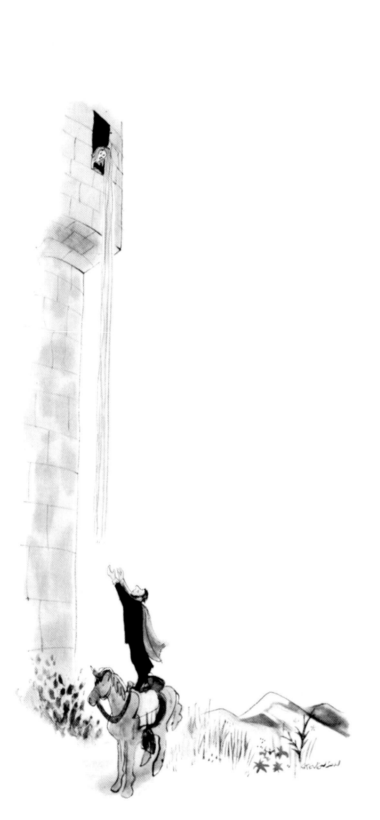

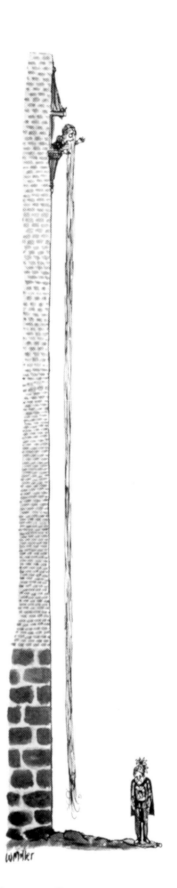

"Could you come back in about six weeks?"

"<u>Now</u> you tell me that you've never been able to even <u>chin</u> yourself!"

LEFT JAMES STEVENSON, MARCH 14, 1964 RIGHT WARREN MILLER, NOVEMBER 25, 1972

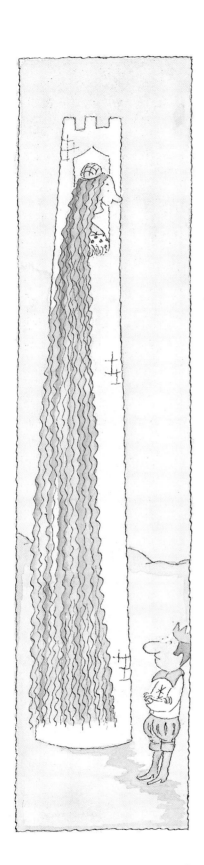

R

"When I'm not having a good hair day,
you'll know."

"Have you noticed how your ends
have the frizzies?"

LEFT VICTORIA ROBERTS, SEPTEMBER 22, 2003   RIGHT AL ROSS, OCTOBER 16, 1971

"We'll take it."

"Location, location, location."

TOP BOB MANKOFF, NOVEMBER 17, 1997   BOTTOM BRUCE KAPLAN, FEBRUARY 28, 1994

"*Well, the down payment has cleared and the paperwork is filed—
as soon as you pee on the lawn, the place is yours.*"

"*I came, I bought, I subdivided.*"

TOP PETE HOLMES, NOVEMBER 5, 2007   BOTTOM MICHAEL MASLIN, JUNE 14, 1999

DOWN PAYMENTS

L*OCATION, LOCATION, LOCATION.* Everyone can repeat the Realtor's motto. But put it in the mouth of a Bruce Kaplan pigeon perched on a skyscraper's ledge, above unseen and unsuspecting pedestrians, and the words assume a wittier perspective. Point of view determines whether a joke lands. On the topic of housing, *The New Yorker*'s resident jesters enjoy taking the position of naïfs who are at the mercy of market forces, building codes, and rampant overcrowding. **Home is where the humor is.** "We'll take it," blurt a pair of overanxious apartment-hunters, so desperate for a place to lay their heads that they'll sign a lease before the floor is finished. Even before the subprime mortgage crisis in 2007, property speculators were popular targets of derision in *The New Yorker*. But alas, there's so much to lampoon and so little room. Cartoonists, who have seen their acreage within the magazine shrink over time, from the full-page spreads of Arno and Addams to the cozy corner niches of today, will continue to squeeze jokes into, and out of, any space that's available. ♦

PETER STEINER, DECEMBER 9, 1996

"It's small, but it's right on the beach."

TOP DANNY SHANAHAN, JUNE 28, 2004 BOTTOM P.C. VEY, SEPTEMBER 23, 1996

"Is it from a mix or from scratch?"

"It's just the architect's model, but I'm very excited."

TOP DANA FRADON, NOVEMBER 26, 1990   BOTTOM LEO CULLUM, NOVEMBER 24, 1997

"*Hi—I'm the bluebird of color-blindness.*"

"*My mom was a Holstein-Friesian, and my dad was the King of Diamonds.*"

TOP DAVID SIPRESS, NOVEMBER 26, 2007   BOTTOM MICHAEL CRAWFORD, JANUARY 12, 2015

"A penny for your thoughts."

"Happy Valentine's Day!"

TOP TOM CHENEY, NOVEMBER 26, 2007   BOTTOM BOB MANKOFF, NOVEMBER 26, 2007

"I don't belong to an organized religion. My religious beliefs are way too disorganized."

"I'm Jewish and Don is Catholic, but we're raising the kids as wolves."

TOP WILLIAM HAEFELI, FEBRUARY 2, 2004   BOTTOM ZACHARY KANIN, APRIL 11, 2011

Politics Finance Religion

"How can I love my enemies when I don't even like my friends?"

TOP WARREN MILLER, APRIL 13, 1987   BOTTOM J.B. HANDELSMAN, MAY 5, 2003

"It's true—we *totally* have the best religion!"

"Have you ever thought about becoming a duck?"

TOP DAVID SIPRESS, JUNE 28, 2010 BOTTOM MATTHEW DIFFEE, NOVEMBER 20, 2000

"It's called monotheism, but it looks like downsizing to me."

"Before we discuss destroying the competition, screwing our customers, and laughing all the way to the bank, let's begin this meeting with a prayer."

TOP CHARLES BARSOTTI, JULY 28, 1997   BOTTOM JACK ZIEGLER, APRIL 19, 2004

"I am so past enlightenment."

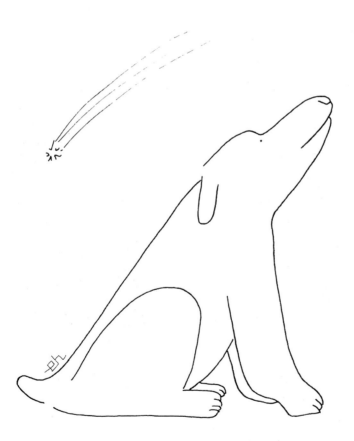

Without Making a Big Deal Out of It,
Dogs Often Question the Existence of an Almighty.

TOP KIM WARP, JUNE 13, 2005   BOTTOM ERIK HILGERDT, OCTOBER 13, 2003

*SEE ALSO *JESUS*, *VIRGIN SACRIFICE*, *ZEUS*

"Good sermon, Reverend, but all that God stuff was pretty far-fetched."

"I couldn't afford health insurance, so I became a Christian Scientist."

TOP BOB MANKOFF, DECEMBER 1, 2003   BOTTOM WILLIAM HAEFELI, MAY 1, 2006

"Très Renaissance!"

"Why, no. I've never thought of putting funny little captions on the bottom."

TOP ED FISHER, JANUARY 15, 1990   BOTTOM ED FISHER, DECEMBER 7, 1998

"Well, let's toss it out the window and see if it flies."

"I'm bored with triptychs. Paint me a quadriptych."

TOP EVERETT OPIE, FEBRUARY 4, 1974   BOTTOM JAMES STEVENSON, MAY 18, 1987

"Give me more angels and make them gladder to see me."

DONALD REILLY, DECEMBER 31, 1966

*"Maybe if we put stone statues in their place,
no one will notice that they've flown away."*

R

Marco Polo Discovers Monosodium Glutamate

TOP GAHAN WILSON, JULY 12, 1999   BOTTOM ELDON DEDINI, MARCH 21, 1988

"I got an A for not smoking."

"Hear ye! Hear ye! I passed English History!"

TOP ROBERT WEBER, JUNE 1, 1998   BOTTOM PERRY BARLOW, JUNE 4, 1938

*"You'll have to do a lot better than this, young man, if you expect to develop
inner resources to cope with your leisure time when you grow up."*

"Tom, this report is very disappointing. What's the matter?"
"I don't know. The teacher just doesn't seem able to teach me anything."

TOP WHITNEY DARROW, JR., NOVEMBER 7, 1964   BOTTOM NANCY FAY, DECEMBER 8, 1928

SO DEGRADING

DREAD. MORTAL DREAD. It grips the hearts of all school-age children at report-card time. Their entire sense of worth comes down to a fistful of letters scrawled on a scrap of paper. But what frightens isn't the opinion of their teachers so much as that of their parents. At no other time in our lives do we experience such angst. That is, until we have school-age children of our own, and that same fistful of letters looms over our entire worth as parents. In this way, **report cards can be viewed as simply another test—of our resilience and creativity in reframing the results.** Faced with explaining the return on his parents' investment, one child advises his businessman father, "It's just a correction. The fundamentals are still good." Give him an A for effort! But the dread remains; cartoonists, after all, know a thing or two about how one's personal record can be blemished by bad marks. ♦

B. Smaller

"*They may be your grades, but they're the return on my investment.*"

BARBARA SMALLER, DECEMBER 23, 2002

"Big deal, an A in math. That would be a D in any other country."

"It's just a correction. The fundamentals are still good."

TOP MIKE TWOHY, MARCH 16, 1998   BOTTOM BERNARD SCHOENBAUM, APRIL 26, 1999

*SEE ALSO EDUCATION, GOOD COP, BAD COP, SCARLET LETTER

"*Those D's are misleading.*"

ROBERT WEBER, FEBRUARY 21, 2000

"I shouldn't, but I'm going to have the garbage."

"We think it's terribly important that you meet the people
responsible for the food you're eating tonight."

TOP MIKE TWOHY, APRIL 2, 2001   BOTTOM EDWARD KOREN, OCTOBER 8, 2007

"Your French is correct, sir—that item is a sneaker filled with gasoline."

"The little sad faces next to some items mean they don't taste very good."

TOP TOM CHENEY, MARCH 10, 2003   BOTTOM LEO CULLUM, APRIL 15, 2002

"I'll have the misspelled 'Ceasar' salad
and the improperly hyphenated veal osso-buco."

"Who ordered the megatelli?"

TOP JACK ZIEGLER, JUNE 3, 2002 BOTTOM CHRISTOPHER WEYANT, SEPTEMBER 6, 2004

"Excuse me—I think there's something wrong with this in a tiny way that no one other than me would ever be able to pinpoint."

TOP MICK STEVENS, APRIL 20, 1987   BOTTOM BRUCE KAPLAN, JUNE 11, 2007

"I'm in a band."

WHEN IT CAME TO OUTSIDE CATERING,
THERE WAS NOTHING TO MATCH THE
UNERRING PRECISION OF ROBIN'S BLADE.

TOP DANNY SHANAHAN, AUGUST 29, 2011   BOTTOM GLEN BAXTER, APRIL 27, 1992

*"You have to declare what you rob from the rich,
but you can deduct what you give to the poor."*

*"Gruel and sassafras tea <u>again</u>! Frankly, we men could be a hell of a lot merrier
if we gave to the poor a little less of that which we take from the rich."*

TOP PAT BYRNES, APRIL 9, 2007   BOTTOM EVERETT OPIE, JUNE 27, 1977

*"To answer your question. Yes, if you shoot an arrow into the air
and it falls to earth you know not where,
you could be liable for any damage it may cause."*

TOP JAMES STEVENSON, SEPTEMBER 19, 1964   BOTTOM MICHAEL MASLIN, OCTOBER 22, 1990

"*Henceforth, we steal from the rich and provide incentives to help the poor steal for themselves.*"

"*How do you expect your men to be merry if you yourself are not merry?*"

TOP PAUL NOTH, AUGUST 10, 2009   BOTTOM AL ROSS, MARCH 12, 1966

Kanin

"If I can't feel love, what was the point of making me so damn good-looking?"

"Sometimes I ask myself, 'Where will it ever end?'"

TOP ZACHARY KANIN, MARCH 2, 2009   BOTTOM CHARLES ADDAMS, FEBRUARY 9, 1946

"Please welcome R70X, our first board member from the ranks of labor."

TOP JACK ZIEGLER, JUNE 2, 2008   BOTTOM HENRY MARTIN, JUNE 13, 1988

TOP TOM CHENEY, OCTOBER 23, 1989 BOTTOM JACK ZIEGLER, OCTOBER 26, 1998

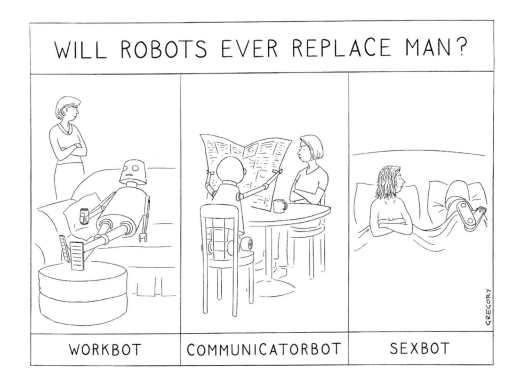

"Well, being single and a robot, I'm able to put in a lot of overtime."

TOP ALEX GREGORY, NOVEMBER 27, 2000   BOTTOM ED FISHER, APRIL 1, 1996

"Oh, hell, Artie. Not another farewell tour."

TOP JACK ZIEGLER, NOVEMBER 17, 2003 BOTTOM DANNY SHANAHAN, AUGUST 6, 1990

"*I haven't been here that long—I'm just a huge ZZ Top fan.*"

"*Two Stones tickets, please, senior discount.*"

TOP MATTHEW DIFFEE, MARCH 3, 2008   BOTTOM PETER STEINER, JANUARY 12, 1998

"Gabe's in the Guitar Hero program at Juilliard."

"Ah, here's some good news, Mr. Gormley.
It seems you've been inducted into the Rock and Roll Hall of Fame."

TOP EMILY FLAKE, FEBRUARY 9, 2009   BOTTOM JACK ZIEGLER, DECEMBER 28, 1992

"Not bad, fellas. Let's do one more take, with more emphasis on tone, harmony, melody, rhythm, composition, lyrics, musicianship, tempo, and originality."

R

MEGADETH COMES FOR THE ARCHBISHOP

TOP TOM CHENEY, JUNE 15, 1998   BOTTOM MICHAEL CRAWFORD, JULY 12, 1993

"Your king said 'Sit!'"

"Hello. You have reached the Palace. If you wish to speak to the King, press '1' now.
If you wish to speak to the Queen, press '2' now.
If you wish to speak to the Chancellor of the Exchequer, press '3' now.
And if you wish to speak to the Minister of Culture—well, hi!"

TOP WILLIAM STEIG, JUNE 5, 1989   BOTTOM JACK ZIEGLER, MARCH 1, 1993

"But when a __woman__ has someone's head cut off she's a bitch."

TOP GAHAN WILSON, JUNE 22, 1987   BOTTOM ALEX GREGORY, JULY 9, 2001

CROWNING GLORY

IN A COUNTRY where royalty is banned, it's funny just how readily we relate to it. We happily identify with the king who fawns over his gift, "Why, this is fit for me!" We snort with derision at the king stewing over the tiny parcel of land belonging to someone else. And we commiserate with the king whose unflinching dog defies his commands, exposing both the limits of his true power and the limitlessness of his self-importance. **Cartoonists are jesters speaking truth to power, hoping our laughter can keep us humble, whatever our pomp or circumstance.** And the truth is, we all entertain, from time to time, the secret desire to be a king or a queen (or, you know, condo-board president), confident that *we* would not let it go to our heads. At times like those, a chuckle over a royal cartoon or two might very well help us *keep* our heads. Long laugh the king. ♦

WARREN MILLER, NOVEMBER 18, 1996

"Castle."

"I'm tired of being Queen. I want to be First Lady."

TOP CHARLES BARSOTTI, SEPTEMBER 2, 1987   BOTTOM JOSEPH FARRIS, APRIL 20, 1987

"It is we."

"Tell me again, Dad, how you started in the mailroom."

TOP CHARLES BARSOTTI, SEPTEMBER 4, 1971   BOTTOM LEO CULLUM, FEBRUARY 13, 1995

"Don't worry, we'll soon have you all sorted out."

"I chuckle acceptingly over my inability to solve Rubik's Cube. That's the kind of person I am."

TOP GAHAN WILSON, MAY 3, 2010   BOTTOM ROBERT WEBER, AUGUST 31, 1981

TOP SAM GROSS, SEPTEMBER 21, 1981   BOTTOM JOHN O'BRIEN, NOVEMBER 22, 2010

NURIT KARLIN, MAY 1, 1978

SAINT PETER
SANDBOXES
SANDCASTLES
SCARLET LETTER
SCIENTISTS IN LAB
SECOND AMENDMENT
SEX
SHARKS
SHOPPING
SISYPHUS
SMILEY FACE
SMOKERS
SNAILS
SNOW WHITE
SNOWMEN
SONG LYRICS
SPACE ALIENS
STANDUP
STATUE OF LIBERTY
STONEHENGE
SUPERHEROES

"We find you acceptable, sir. You will be issued a halo, a set of wings, and an honorary doctorate in the subject of your choice."

"The old pearly gates looked nice, but they were hell to maintain."

TOP J.B. HANDELSMAN, APRIL 8, 1972   BOTTOM MIKE TWOHY, AUGUST 17, 1998

*"You're not coming up on my computer.
How long did you say you've been dead?"*

*"And twelve: How did you learn about us—(a) church,
(b) synagogue, (c) family member, (d) word of mouth?"*

TOP MICHAEL MASLIN, APRIL 21, 1997   BOTTOM HENRY MARTIN, DECEMBER 15, 1997

"I'd like to congratulate you on dying with dignity."

J.B. HANDELSMAN, AUGUST 4, 1997

"St. Peter retired some time back. I'm St. Bill."

"I don't think so."

TOP MICK STEVENS, MARCH 2, 1992   BOTTOM MICK STEVENS, JUNE 15, 1998

"It's full of sand."

"By the time I develop a true understanding of sand,
I'll probably be forced into some sort of organized sports."

TOP PETER MUELLER, JULY 16, 2001   BOTTOM P.C. VEY, SEPTEMBER 11, 2006

*"I'm focusing less on girls and more on accumulating
the things girls will eventually want."*

"It turns out I just wasted the whole morning networking with a dog."

TOP C. COVERT DARBYSHIRE, SEPTEMBER 13, 2004   BOTTOM ZACHARY KANIN, APRIL 20, 2009

"He doesn't have to worry about his preschool placement—he interviews well."

"Come pick me up. This is going nowhere."

TOP BARBARA SMALLER, JULY 12, 1999 BOTTOM ELDON DEDINI, APRIL 2, 2001

*SEE ALSO DESERT ISLAND, HEAT WAVES, WATER COOLER

TOP BARNEY TOBEY, SEPTEMBER 5, 1959 BOTTOM JACK ZIEGLER, MAY 8, 2000

*"We're a great team, Sash—you with your small and large motor skills,
me with my spatial awareness and hand-eye coördination."*

TOP BRUCE KAPLAN, AUGUST 10, 1998   BOTTOM EDWARD KOREN, JULY 25, 1988

"City kids."

"Dad, would you please go back to doing the parenting,
so that I can do some of the childing for a couple of minutes?"

TOP HARRY BLISS, AUGUST 9, 1999   BOTTOM JACK ZIEGLER, AUGUST 22, 1988

"*I hope we can flip it before the tide comes in.*"

TOP JAMES STEVENSON, AUGUST 7, 1978   BOTTOM ALEX GREGORY, FEBRUARY 6, 2006

"We swam. We made sand castles. I'm sorry, Michael—
I thought you understood that this was just a summer thing."

TOP CHARLES ADDAMS, AUGUST 3, 1987   BOTTOM CHRISTOPHER WEYANT, SEPTEMBER 2, 2002

TOP SAM GROSS, JUNE 26, 1995   BOTTOM PAT BYRNES, JUNE 8, 2009

*SEE ALSO ADULTERY, DIVORCE, WRITERS

"Why can't you be more like little Hester Prynne?
She's getting straight A's."

TOP SAM GROSS, JUNE 22, 1998   BOTTOM SAM GROSS, NOVEMBER 23, 1998

"We're isolating the obesity gene, but only to make fun of it."

"That's Dr. Arnold Moore. He's conducting an experiment to test the theory that most great scientific discoveries were hit on by accident."

TOP PAUL NOTH, MAY 11, 2009   BOTTOM SYDNEY HOFF, SEPTEMBER 28, 1957

"I'll thank you to stop referring to my research, Whatley, as sci-fi."

"We're in our lab coats. Now what?"

TOP JAMES STEVENSON, JULY 22, 1985 BOTTOM VICTORIA ROBERTS, DECEMBER 28, 1998

"Looks like Wesselman's hit on something interesting."

CHARLES ADDAMS, JUNE 18, 1955

*SEE ALSO EUREKA, INVENTIONS, LIGHT BULB IDEA

"I see by the current issue of 'Lab News,' Ridgeway, that you've been working for the last twenty years on the same problem I've been working on for the last twenty years."

"And I say pull the plug while we still can."

TOP EVERETT OPIE, JANUARY 5, 1976   BOTTOM LEE LORENZ, NOVEMBER 18, 2002

"*How very exciting! I have never before met a Second Amendment lawyer.*"

"*You know, if she weren't part of a well-regulated militia I'd be a little nervous.*"

TOP J.B. HANDELSMAN, MAY 29, 1989   BOTTOM BOB MANKOFF, JUNE 14, 1999

THE N.R.A.'s WRITTEN TEST FOR A GUN LICENSE

① My favorite kind of gun is a _____,
because _____.

② When I carry a gun, I feel _____, and
the bigger the gun the more _____ I feel.

③ My favorite part of shooting is when ____
_____
_____.

④ If a robber tried to rob me, I'd shoot
him in the _____.

⑤ In my fantasies, the three people I'd most
like to blow away are _____,
_____, and _____.

⑥ Guns are like rolls of Scotch tape. There should
be at least ___ in every room of the house.

⑦ I'm all for gun safety, but _____
_____
_____
_____
_____ .(Use reverse side if necessary.)

⑧ People who don't like guns are _____
and ought to be _____.

R. Chast

ROZ CHAST, AUGUST 2, 1999

"A well-regulated militia being necessary to the security of a free state, we need cheap, available handguns."

"Trust me. It's not a God-given right."

TOP PETER STEINER, MARCH 6, 2000   BOTTOM SAM GROSS, OCTOBER 9, 2000

*SEE ALSO AMERICAN HISTORY, DUELS, GUNS

"For a militia, he's not very well regulated."

TOP DEAN VIETOR, JUNE 13, 1988   BOTTOM CHRISTOPHER WEYANT, SEPTEMBER 1, 2014

"Why, you're right. Tonight isn't reading night, tonight is sex night."

"To quote my broker, 'Past results are no guarantee of future performance.'"

TOP BOB MANKOFF, JANUARY 18, 1993   BOTTOM J.C. DUFFY, APRIL 22, 2002

"It's a shame there isn't a pill to stimulate conversation."

"Was it 'meh' for you, too?"

TOP ALEX GREGORY, MAY 24, 2004   BOTTOM HARRY BLISS, FEBRUARY 13, 2017

"*Will you call me?*"

"*So you're having trouble conceiving. Have you tried sex?*"

TOP CHARLES BARSOTTI, APRIL 10, 1995 MIDDLE DREW DERNAVICH, OCTOBER 17, 2005 BOTTOM MICHAEL SHAW, DECEMBER 19, 2005

"We rarely watch television. Most of our free time is devoted to sex."

ROBERT WEBER, JULY 20, 1998

ARIEL MOLVIG, APRIL 5, 2010

CARNAL KNOWLEDGE

BIRDS DO IT, BEES DO IT, even cartoonists do it. Or at least we think about it. A lot. Our culture romanticizes and glamorizes sex. It gets used to sell everything from toothpaste to power tools. **Count on cartoonists, though, to spoil the mood.** Some magazines submit to male fantasies in their illustrations, but *The New Yorker* has always preferred a different position. When a man asks his wife, "Was it 'meh' for you too?," or a couple mixes up reading night with sex night, their anticlimax is our climax. The sheets get pulled out from under our phantasms; we are thrust into naked reality. And the laughter comes. Naturally. For all of our culture's sniggering sex worship, it's this kind of insight that touches us. And isn't that the most seductive, and elusive, thing about sex? A cozy relationship with reality has always been one of the two great ways in which a *New Yorker* sex cartoon is much closer to sex itself than its more pornographic counterparts. The other is that it's over too fast. ◆

"We usually have a light breakfast,
then a feeding frenzy in the early afternoon, and that's it for the day."

"You've got a bit of thong caught between your front teeth."

TOP LEO CULLUM, JULY 15, 1991   BOTTOM NICK DOWNES, JULY 31, 2000

"It's a great school, but it wasn't my first choice."

"To be perfectly honest, I've never ripped into anything
that wasn't begging to be ripped into."

TOP DANNY SHANAHAN, JUNE 14, 2010   BOTTOM JACK ZIEGLER, SEPTEMBER 10, 2001

"*What you need to watch is the snacking between frenzies.*"

"*I start every diet with the best intentions,
but it goes to hell as soon as I sense blood in the water.*"

"*Trust me, you're going to be very happy you
brought along legal representation.*"

TOP DANNY SHANAHAN, MAY 22, 2006 MIDDLE CHARLES BARSOTTI, DECEMBER 27, 1999 BOTTOM KIM WARP, AUGUST 9, 2010

*SEE ALSO DENTISTRY, SMILEY FACE

"There's your problem."

"I guess this is me."

TOP FARLEY KATZ, FEBRUARY 4, 2008   BOTTOM CHRISTOPHER WEYANT, NOVEMBER 14, 2005

"Main floor, aisle six, ladies' scarves. Shopper down."

"I'm looking for something slightly more perfect."

TOP JACK ZIEGLER, DECEMBER 21, 1998   BOTTOM BRUCE KAPLAN, MARCH 20, 2006

"What would you suggest that would make
a nine-year-old boy's mother happy?"

"I should have bought more crap."

TOP BARBARA SMALLER, MAY 23, 2005   BOTTOM ERIC LEWIS, NOVEMBER 18, 2002

*"Sorry, sir, but the high-quality items you're used to are no longer made.
We can only remind you of them, by charging high prices for the current stuff."*

TOP ED FISHER, OCTOBER 19, 1992 BOTTOM MATTHEW DIFFEE, APRIL 11, 2005

"*Finally! Cheap is the new black!*"

"*She's a little traumatized—this is her first Wal-Mart.*"

TOP CAROLITA JOHNSON, MARCH 16, 2009   BOTTOM EDWARD KOREN, DECEMBER 8, 1997

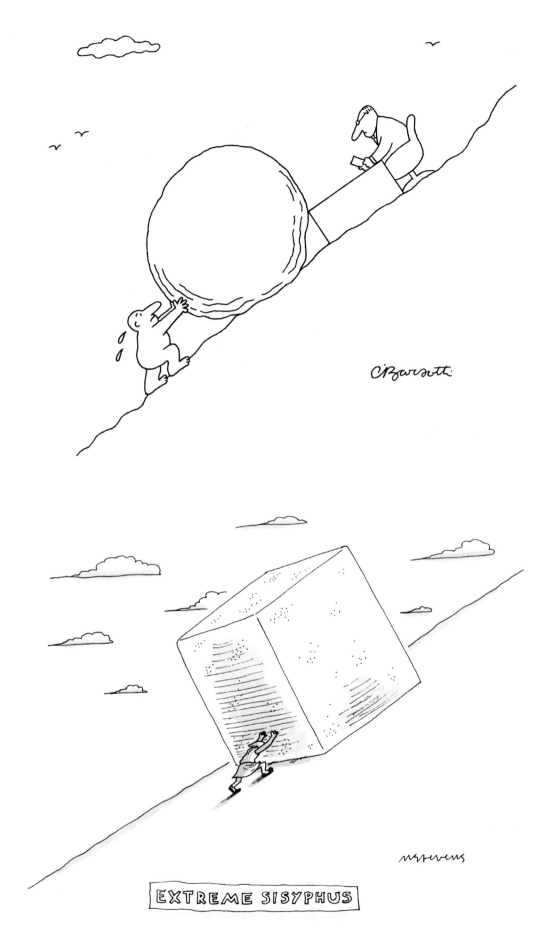

EXTREME SISYPHUS

TOP CHARLES BARSOTTI, DECEMBER 8, 2008   BOTTOM MICK STEVENS, JANUARY 2, 2012

"*Can't you ever relax?*"

TOP CHRISTOPHER WEYANT, NOVEMBER 29, 2010 BOTTOM CHRISTOPHER WEYANT, JUNE 17, 2002

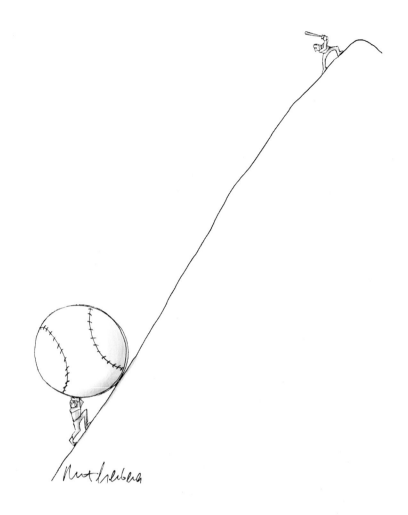

"Hey, Sisyphus, when you've got a minute
I'd like to discuss this progress report with you."

TOP MORT GERBERG, JULY 6, 2009 BOTTOM ZACHARY KANIN, JUNE 1, 2009

ROZ CHAST, SEPTEMBER 22, 2008

THE RETURN OF GUARDED OPTIMISM

TOP JACK ZIEGLER, JUNE 1, 2009   BOTTOM LEO CULLUM, DECEMBER 20, 1993

"Doesn't he seem a little old for her?"

TOP BRUCE KAPLAN, MARCH 14, 2011   BOTTOM WARREN MILLER, DECEMBER 1, 1997

NATIONAL TOBACCO INSTITUTE

MANKOFF

"Love it! 'People of smoke' instead of 'Smokers.'"

"Do you think this would have happened even if we weren't the last two smokers in the office?"

TOP BOB MANKOFF, AUGUST 23, 1993   BOTTOM WILLIAM HAMILTON, JANUARY 31, 1994

"I'm going back inside to get some air."

TOP TOM CHENEY, JULY 17, 1995   BOTTOM DAVID SIPRESS, MAY 19, 2003

"You're welcome, but I'm afraid your cigar is not."

TOP EDWARD KOREN, NOVEMBER 15, 1999   BOTTOM DONALD REILLY, DECEMBER 19, 1983

"Look, fella—can't you see this is an executive smokers' group?"

TOP FRANK MODELL, DECEMBER 16, 1967   BOTTOM WILLIAM HAMILTON, SEPTEMBER 15, 1997

"Remember, not one word about his foreclosure."

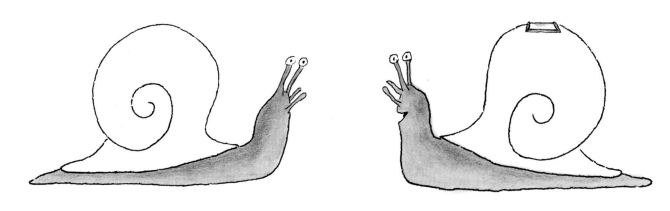

"I put in a skylight and it's made a world of difference."

S. GROSS

ESCARGOT   ESCARGOING   ESCARGONE

TOP TOM CHENEY, SEPTEMBER 24, 2007   MIDDLE SAM GROSS, OCTOBER 17, 2005   BOTTOM ARIEL MOLVIG, FEBRUARY 25, 2008

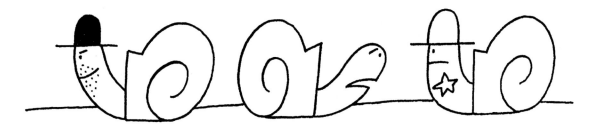

CBarsotti

"He's long gone, sheriff—you'll never catch him."

S.GROSS

"I don't care if she is a tape dispenser. I love her."

CBarsotti

"Well, I want to talk."

TOP CHARLES BARSOTTI, FEBRUARY 21, 2000   MIDDLE SAM GROSS, NOVEMBER 30, 1998   BOTTOM CHARLES BARSOTTI, DECEMBER 10, 2001

"Why, yes, my dear—it is organic."

"Let's get Junkie—he'll know what to do!"

TOP HARRY BLISS, OCTOBER 20, 2008   BOTTOM DANNY SHANAHAN, SEPTEMBER 18, 2006

"How many in your party?"

"And if she doesn't file?"

TOP JAMES STEVENSON, FEBRUARY 26, 1990   BOTTOM DANNY SHANAHAN, APRIL 15, 1991

SNOW WHITE AND HER SEVEN PEOPLE

"There was an eighth dwarf, named Scuzzy, but we killed him."

TOP ROZ CHAST, MARCH 17, 2008 BOTTOM DONALD REILLY, SEPTEMBER 6, 1993

"Who is the fairest one of all, and state your sources!"

*Snow White and the Wicked Queen submit the
fairness question to binding arbitration.*

TOP ED FISHER, DECEMBER 10, 1984   BOTTOM LEE LORENZ, JANUARY 21, 1991

THE SNOWS OF YESTERYEAR: THIRTIES, FORTIES, FIFTIES

Front row: 1930, 1931, 1933, 1934, 1935, 1936, 1938, 1939
Second row: 1941, 1942, 1943, 1944, 1945, 1946, 1947, 1948, 1949
Back row: 1950, 1951, 1952, 1954, 1955, 1956, 1957, 1959
Missing: 1932, 1937, 1940, 1953, 1958

"Nobody told me it was formal!"

TOP HENRY MARTIN, MARCH 6, 1989   BOTTOM DANNY SHANAHAN, MARCH 5, 2001

"*Well, hello there yourself!*"

"*Nobody move! I think I lost an eye.*"

TOP GAHAN WILSON, MARCH 12, 2007　BOTTOM DANNY SHANAHAN, DECEMBER 22, 1997

MORT GERBERG, FEBRUARY 3, 1997

A MIND OF WINTER

WHY ARE SNOWMEN funny? Sigmund Freud, in his classic "Jokes and Their Relation to the Unconscious," says that laughter releases nervous energy. Basically, the only reason a person laughs is because the alternative is to face some horrific secret or, in this case, the fear of melting into oblivion. So perhaps snowmen are funny because we are *not* snowmen: **here today, puddle tomorrow.**

Or, perhaps snowmen are funny because of the happiness that obsolete visual archetypes give us. Like the top hat, which nobody wears anymore. It's just so lovely to see it there. The hat evokes all those black-and-white comedies set in some mythical version of Manhattan where even New Yorkers have British accents. We laugh because Frosty's got on his top hat. And because we realize that Frosty's *doomed*.

Oh, come on, it's *funny*. Still, you have to wonder what exactly Freud would have said about snowmen. Starting with the carrot. ♦

*"We could reshape your nose with conventional surgery,
but I'm going to suggest something radical."*

*"I'll have the bourbon hot toddy." "Make that two."
"Let's see, I'll have a Kahlua and coffee." "I'll have a hot buttered rum."
"And bring me an Irish coffee, please."*

TOP LEO CULLUM, JANUARY 26, 1998 BOTTOM HENRY MARTIN, JANUARY 11, 1999

TOP WILLIAM O'BRIAN, DECEMBER 31, 1966   BOTTOM ANTHONY TABER, JANUARY 12, 1981

"It was I, Glenda. I wrote the book of love."

"You do the hokey-pokey and you turn yourself around—
that's what it's all about."

TOP LEO CULLUM, JUNE 26, 1995   BOTTOM BRUCE KAPLAN, NOVEMBER 22, 1999

"While you were out, Stevie Wonder just called to say he loves you."

"I see you've flown around the world in a plane, and settled revolutions in Spain.
Around a golf course you're under par. Metro-Goldwyn has asked you to star.
Very impressive, I must admit, but we're looking for someone with marketing experience."

TOP BOB MANKOFF, MAY 27, 1985   BOTTOM J.B. HANDELSMAN, OCTOBER 12, 1987

DREAM ON

"I'm dreaming of a white Christmas."

"Oops! There goes another rubber-tree plant!"

TOP BOB MANKOFF, NOVEMBER 25, 1991 BOTTOM VICTORIA ROBERTS, MAY 13, 1996

"C'mon, Sugar,
take a walk on the mild side."

"It's beginning to look a lot like Christmas."

"My daddy's rich and my ma is good-lookin',
but I'm a mess."

TOP MARISA ACOCELLA, AUGUST 23, 1999 MIDDLE GEORGE BOOTH, DECEMBER 13, 1999 BOTTOM ROBERT WEBER, APRIL 26, 1999

"I hope my address to the American Astronomical Society
will bring us the credibility we've been seeking."

"For some reason the earthlings are not regarding us
with the level of awe we were told to expect."

TOP HENRY MARTIN, APRIL 23, 1990   BOTTOM ROBERT LEIGHTON, DECEMBER 9, 2002

*"You can't keep comparing yourself to those skinny
little aliens you see in movies."*

*"Why have we come? Because only Earth offers the rock-bottom prices and wide selection of
men's, women's, and children's clothing in the styles and sizes we're looking for."*

TOP BRUCE KAPLAN, SEPTEMBER 17, 2001   BOTTOM MICHAEL MASLIN, AUGUST 4, 1997

"They seem friendly enough so far."

"I assure you, Madam, if any such creatures as you describe really existed,
we would be the first to know about it."

TOP MICK STEVENS, FEBRUARY 23, 2009   BOTTOM ALAN DUNN, JUNE 4, 1966

*SEE ALSO IMMIGRATION, U.F.O.s

"Take us to Lady Gaga."

INTELLIGENT BEINGS FROM OUTER SPACE

TOP DAVID SIPRESS, MARCH 29, 2010   BOTTOM MICK STEVENS, FEBRUARY 4, 1991

"*And that was my day at the office.*
Thanks, Alice, you've been a great audience!"

"*I just flew in from the Coast. Boy, are my references tired.*"

TOP MICK STEVENS, APRIL 2, 1990   BOTTOM BRUCE KAPLAN, FEBRUARY 23, 1998

*"Now is the part of the show when we ask the audience
to shout out some random numbers."*

"I don't sing. I do standup."

TOP DREW DERNAVICH, FEBRUARY 11, 2008 BOTTOM SAM GROSS, JANUARY 18, 1999

(Official Government Photo)
Nov. 28 (UPI)—At his office in the capital city, the world's
most powerful dictator greets the world's funniest standup comic.

TOP LEO CULLUM, DECEMBER 5, 1988 BOTTOM JACK ZIEGLER, DECEMBER 4, 1978

STANDUP COMIC DOING PRO-BONO WORK IN ISOLATED RURAL AREA

"Whew! Tough crowd."

TOP SIDNEY HARRIS, JULY 31, 1989   BOTTOM JACK ZIEGLER, MAY 19, 2003

*"Well, it all depends.
Where are these huddled masses coming from?"*

TOP J.B. HANDELSMAN, JUNE 8, 1992   BOTTOM MISCHA RICHTER, AUGUST 8, 1977

CONDOMANIA

BOB MANKOFF, APRIL 30, 1984

"He's fallen in love with her."

"To the lady in the harbor."

TOP JOSEPH FARRIS, MARCH 18, 1967   BOTTOM BOB MANKOFF, DECEMBER 2, 1985

"Have you no sense of propriety?"

"Witness will confine herself to answering counsel's questions,
and refrain from giving opinions as to constitutionality and the like."

TOP JOSEPH FARRIS, MARCH 1, 1969   BOTTOM J.B. HANDELSMAN, JULY 22, 1991

*"Now that we can tell time,
I'd like to suggest that we begin imposing deadlines."*

TOP TOM CHENEY, OCTOBER 10, 2005   BOTTOM SAM GROSS, MAY 9, 1994

STONEHENGE DECODED

TOP DAVID SIPRESS, JULY 25, 2011 BOTTOM LEE LORENZ, FEBRUARY 1, 2010

"Well, we've done it, but don't ask me how."

WILLIAM O'BRIAN, MAY 6, 1961

*SEE ALSO EASTER ISLAND, PYRAMIDS, VIRGIN SACRIFICE

"Like the concept. Like the whole thing. But take out the arches."

"It's a pity they had to stop work on the new mall."

TOP WARREN MILLER, JUNE 28, 1976 BOTTOM TOM CHENEY, JANUARY 6, 2003

"Why, yes, I do have buns of steel."

"Do you have any references besides Batman?"

TOP BRUCE KAPLAN, AUGUST 23, 1993   BOTTOM MORT GERBERG, JULY 7, 1997

"Well, your jersey damn sure wasn't inside out
when you left home this morning."

TOP CHARLES BARSOTTI, MAY 29, 1989   BOTTOM DANNY SHANAHAN, SEPTEMBER 11, 1989

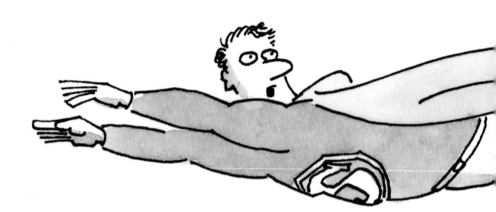

UP, UP, AND AWAY

THE SECOND WORLD WAR was a big inconvenience for DC Comics, as the United States entered into it two years after the publishers delivered Superman into the arms of Ma and Pa Kent. The comic's creators couldn't ignore the war, but if they sent Superman overseas, he'd kick the asses of Hitler, Mussolini, and Hirohito and be back in time to file the afternoon edition of the *Daily Planet*. The solution was to have Clark Kent fail his induction exam. During the eye test, he mistakenly used his X-ray vision, looking through the wall at the chart in the next room.

Superheroes are idiots with magical powers who are, usually, taken way too seriously. That makes them perfect targets for gags. Plus, they're already cartoons! Cartoonists show us Batman inserting his ATM card upside down or adulterous Superman making a bush-league mistake that the wife, of course, notices ("Your jersey damn sure wasn't inside out when you left home this morning!"). More powerful than a locomotive, too stupid to pass an eye exam. ♦

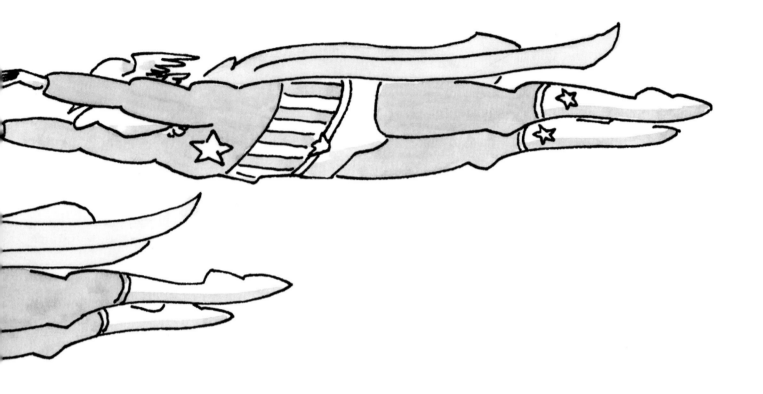

"Yes, but what I really want to do is write children's books."

TOP JACK ZIEGLER, NOVEMBER 8, 2004

"I'm letting my nemesis define me."

TOP ARIEL MOLVIG, AUGUST 25, 2008 BOTTOM LEO CULLUM, APRIL 14, 2008

"Hold on—I was putting my card in upside down."

DANNY SHANAHAN, OCTOBER 24, 1994

TOM HACHTMAN, SEPTEMBER 20, 1999

TALENT AGENTS

TAXES

TENNIS

THE THINKER

THE THREE MONKEYS

THINKING OUTSIDE THE BOX

THREE LITTLE PIGS

TOASTERS

TOMBSTONES

TORTOISE & THE HARE

TOUPEES

TROJAN HORSE

TRUMP

TRUTH

TUNNEL OF LOVE

TURTLES

TWITTER

Star running-back "Zigzag" Johnson, his lawyer,
and his agent score from the 27-yard line.

TOP AL ROSS, SEPTEMBER 16, 1991   BOTTOM DEAN VIETOR, NOVEMBER 7, 1988

"Stop! He's my agent!"

"It's your agent. Everyone wants a piece of you."

TOP SAM GROSS, JANUARY 21, 2002   BOTTOM MIKE TWOHY, JANUARY 22, 1996

"He killed in rehab."

"We've come up with an idea for getting your stuff into caves everywhere."

TOP DANNY SHANAHAN, NOVEMBER 15, 1999   BOTTOM DONALD REILLY, DECEMBER 10, 1990

"Yeah, he's in rehab, but for the right role I can spring him."

"Yeah, yeah, I know. You need a Laurence Fishburne-Forest Whitaker-James Earl Jones type."

TOP CHARLES BARSOTTI, AUGUST 19, 1996 BOTTOM CHARLES BARSOTTI, APRIL 29, 1996

"It was Socrates, wasn't it, who said, 'The unexamined life is not worth living'?"

TOP BENJAMIN SCHWARTZ, MARCH 16, 2015   BOTTOM LEO CULLUM, APRIL 5, 1993

"Do you want to do that hilarious thing where we read
the itemized deductions and then say 'in bed'?"

"Other folks have to pay taxes, too, Mr. Herndon, so would you please spare us the dramatics!"

TOP DREW DERNAVICH, APRIL 19, 2004   BOTTOM GEORGE BOOTH, MARCH 18, 1972

DEATH, TAXES & MY UROLOGIST, DR. AARON KATZ

TOP MICK STEVENS, APRIL 7, 1986 MIDDLE LEE LORENZ, APRIL 5, 2010 BOTTOM BOB ECKSTEIN, APRIL 13, 2015

*SEE ALSO ACCOUNTANTS, DEPRESSION, TRUMP

"Audit him—but make it look like an accident."

*"Owing to an unforeseen dip in the fiefdom's population,
we regret that we must once again raise taxes."*

TOP CHRISTOPHER WEYANT, MAY 27, 2013   BOTTOM JACK ZIEGLER, NOVEMBER 2, 2015

"As in real life, Avery, you're only as good as your second serve."

"Insurance, anyone?"

TOP MORT GERBERG, APRIL 22, 1985 BOTTOM MICK STEVENS, MARCH 23, 1992

"Nick is in here, pondering his backhand."

*"Look, I didn't come down here to work on our relationship.
I came here to work on my backhand."*

TOP EDWARD KOREN, JULY 4, 1988   BOTTOM LEE LORENZ, JUNE 16, 1986

"Advantage, Mom."

"It's kind of a shame, really. Before tennis they used to be the best of friends."

TOP BOB MANKOFF, SEPTEMBER 17, 1990   BOTTOM WARREN MILLER, AUGUST 1, 1988

"And the score remains unchanged."

*"His serve is excellent, his forehand is strong, his backhand
and net game are coming along well, but he needs a louder grunt."*

TOP ZACHARY KANIN, SEPTEMBER 17, 2007   BOTTOM JAMES STEVENSON, AUGUST 13, 1990

THE RETHINKER

"I know the type. All you'd ever get out of him would be 'We can't afford it'!"

TOP ARNIE LEVIN, JANUARY 5, 1981   BOTTOM L.H. SIGGS, AUGUST 30, 1952

"Personally, I'm a doer."

TOP MISCHA RICHTER, AUGUST 27, 1955   BOTTOM MIKE TWOHY, APRIL 28, 1997

PENNY FOR YOUR THOUGHTS

A RT MAKES YOU FEEL. But sometimes it also makes you think. And the work of art that has made more people think than perhaps any other is Rodin's "The Thinker." It is a six-foot-high bronze embodiment of the question **"Have you ever wondered what someone else is thinking?"** Cartoonists live for such thoughts. So they've employed this sculpture to think about how some people think of themselves as thinkers and others as doers. They have pondered the sculptor thinking vainly while awaiting an inspiration that is all too clear to us. They have thought about the expression of other styles of thought, such as rethinking wor groupthink. And they have devoted considerable thought to what "The Thinker" himself might be thinking. Is he wondering why he wasn't cast as Rodin's *second*-most famous sculpture, "The Kiss," instead? Or is he lost in more abstract thoughts—expressed, of course, as abstract sculpture? Or is he simply thinking too much? Cartoonists, at least, cannot overthink "The Thinker." And as long as there are thoughts left to think, cartoonists will continue to ink. ◆

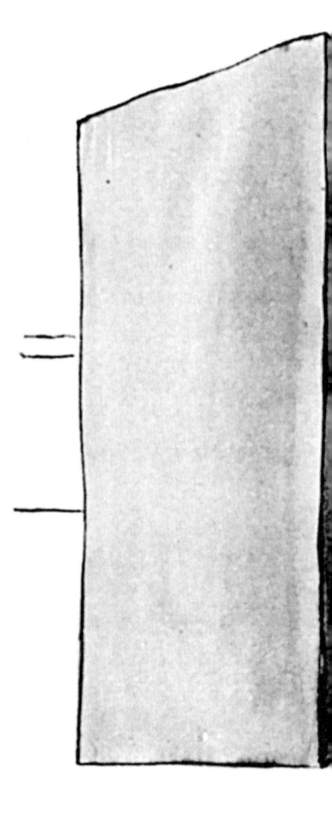

ANATOL KOVARSKY, OCTOBER 11, 1958

HERBERT GOLDBERG, DECEMBER 9, 1974

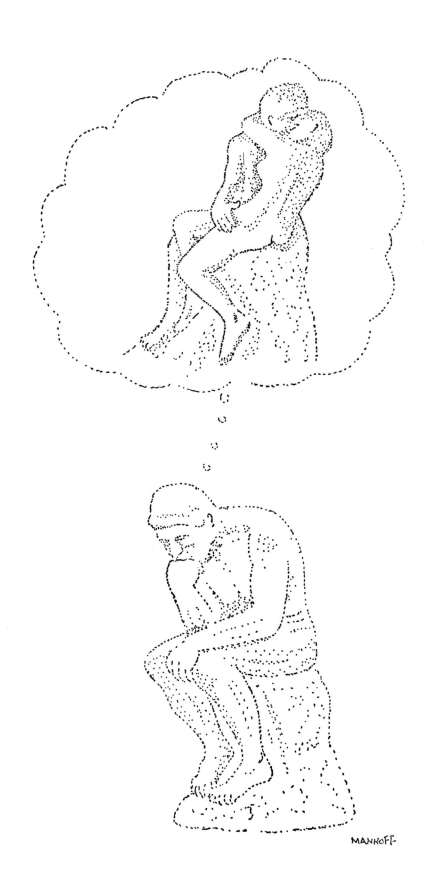

BOB MANKOFF, JUNE 29, 1981

"Believe me, you're just thinking about it too much."

TOP CHARLES ADDAMS, DECEMBER 10, 1984   BOTTOM BOB MANKOFF, NOVEMBER 30, 1998

THE THINKER *

*SEE ALSO FAMOUS PAINTERS & PAINTINGS, MEDITATION, NUDISM

TOP WILLIAM STEIG, MARCH 27, 1965   BOTTOM ARNIE LEVIN, AUGUST 8, 1988

"Next time you want information, don't send up three monkeys!"

TOP ARNIE LEVIN, MAY 7, 1979   BOTTOM ALAN DUNN, JUNE 27, 1959

TOP ARNIE LEVIN, JANUARY 14, 1980   MIDDLE ED ARNO, NOVEMBER 23, 1981   BOTTOM WARREN MILLER, JANUARY 9, 1984

"He's very busy right now. He's thinking his way out of a box."

"Never, ever, think outside the box."

TOP ROBERT WEBER, MARCH 10, 1975   BOTTOM LEO CULLUM, NOVEMBER 30, 1998

"Actually, I got some pretty good ideas when I was in the box."

"We also have urns, if you want to think outside the box."

TOP SAM GROSS, MAY 8, 2006   BOTTOM MIKE TWOHY, AUGUST 18, 2003

"I'm not huffing and puffing. I'm foreclosing."

TOP ROZ CHAST, OCTOBER 5, 2009 BOTTOM CHRISTOPHER WEYANT, APRIL 28, 2008

*SEE ALSO ARCHITECTURE, BEDTIME STORIES, LET ME THROUGH

*"He's big, all right, and he's definitely a wolf,
but it'll be up to a jury to decide whether or not he's bad."*

"I don't think good huffing and puffing can be taught."

TOP MICHAEL MASLIN, FEBRUARY 1, 1999   BOTTOM BRUCE KAPLAN, APRIL 23, 2001

"And they say electric cars aren't practical."

"Ah, just the person I was looking for."

TOP ROBERT WEBER, JANUARY 25, 1999   BOTTOM P.C. VEY, OCTOBER 3, 2011

THE COMPLETE HISTORY OF TOAST

MUELLER

THE FINAL ALL-TOAST SUPPER AT APARTMENT 5-B

TOP PETER MUELLER, MARCH 19, 2001   BOTTOM JACK ZIEGLER, MARCH 3, 2003

THE MAYOR ED KOCH TOASTER

THE JOHN AND YOKO MODEL

CHARLIE'S ANGELS

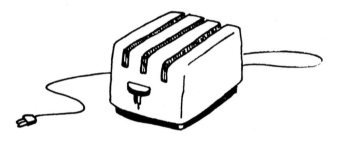

THE FOUR HORSEMEN OF THE APOCALYPSE

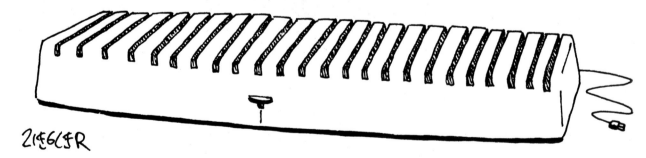

AND THE NEW MILFORD, CONNECTICUT, VOLUNTEER FIRE DEPARTMENT
AND THEIR FAMILIES

JACK ZIEGLER, APRIL 14, 1980

"At long last, Wyatt, our dream has come true and we are within reach of the legendary toast fields of the Sierra Madre."

TOP JACK ZIEGLER, NOVEMBER 23, 2009   BOTTOM JACK ZIEGLER, APRIL 18, 2005

MANKOFF

TOP BOB MANKOFF, SEPTEMBER 2, 1985 BOTTOM STAN HUNT, APRIL 1, 1967

TOP MICHAEL MASLIN, JULY 21, 1997   BOTTOM TOM CHENEY, FEBRUARY 8, 1993

TOP P.C. VEY, SEPTEMBER 28, 2009   BOTTOM BARBARA SMALLER, APRIL 24, 2000

"Could you kindly pick up the tempo a bit?"

"Hey, it's not a race."

TOP BERNARD SCHOENBAUM, MARCH 2, 1992   BOTTOM DANNY SHANAHAN, NOVEMBER 28, 2005

TOP MORT GERBERG, OCTOBER 15, 1990   BOTTOM J.P. RINI, MAY 7, 1990

"After I won, I came all unglued."

TOP MISCHA RICHTER, MARCH 4, 1991   BOTTOM VICTORIA ROBERTS, AUGUST 7, 1995

"No, thanks. I'm in training."

TOP ARNIE LEVIN, AUGUST 21, 2000   BOTTOM MICK STEVENS, SEPTEMBER 23, 1991

"Toupee!"

"Don't mention hair loss."

TOP SAM GROSS, AUGUST 21, 2000 BOTTOM DANNY SHANAHAN, AUGUST 17, 1992

"Now, if I were you I'd lose some weight, get contact lenses, put lifts in my shoes, wear a toupee, grow a moustache, and start smoking a pipe."

"Your Honor, I ask you—is this the toupee of a successful adulterer?"

TOP BOB MANKOFF, APRIL 20, 1987 BOTTOM J.C. DUFFY, OCTOBER 16, 2000

"How do we know it's not full of consultants?"

"I like the concept if we can do it with no new taxes."

TOP CHRISTOPHER WEYANT, JULY 4, 2011   BOTTOM DANA FRADON, OCTOBER 23, 1989

"I can't just leave it—somebody has to sign for it."

INSIDE JOB

HERE'S A TEST of your cartoon I.Q.: Which Ancient Greece setup provides a visual that's instantly recognizable (not to mention funny-looking)?

The Face That Launched a Thousand Ships
The Horse That Fooled a Thousand Dopes

Long after Helen and all that foolishness she caused is long forgotten, the Trojan Horse will be used in gag cartoons. "Beware of Greeks bearing gifts"? Beware of *anyone* bearing gifts! At its heart, the Trojan Horse gag draws on the sting we've all felt when our delight at a beautifully wrapped gift is swiftly replaced, once the ribbon is cut and the wrapping's on the floor, by other emotions. Husband buys wife vacuum cleaner; wife buys husband gym membership. *How could I ever have opened the front gate and let that idiot into my life?* Another reason that the Trojan Horse gag will never die: the dang thing always looks like a gigantic pull-toy. Where's the gigantic toddler? ♦

"*Special Forces.*"

DANA FRADON, NOVEMBER 11, 2002

"You're right, sir—it is cute. But the last time we let one of these things in the entire kingdom was overrun with ticks, mites, and fleas."

JACK ZIEGLER, FEBRUARY 13, 2006

*SEE ALSO GREEK MYTHOLOGY, HORSE COSTUME, WAR

"This is a hell of a time to tell me you have claustrophobia."

"We're going to try to negotiate first."

TOP ALAIN, JANUARY 2, 1960   BOTTOM DANA FRADON, NOVEMBER 30, 1992

"Look, just nuke them and build something terrific."

"I remember when I was the Donald!"

TOP PAUL NOTH, SEPTEMBER 28, 2015 BOTTOM LEE LORENZ, AUGUST 23, 1993

*"Last night, I dreamed I was Donald Trump
and I built a seven-story building right here in Eagle Falls."*

TOP LIAM WALSH, APRIL 25, 2016   BOTTOM JAMES STEVENSON, DECEMBER 9, 1985

"You may be asking for trouble, Ernie."

*"You can eat the one marshmallow right now, or, if you wait fifteen minutes,
I'll give you two marshmallows and swear you in as President of the United States."*

TOP JAMES STEVENSON, APRIL 23, 1990   BOTTOM PAUL NOTH, JANUARY 23, 2017

J.C. DUFFY, NOVEMBER 29, 1999

"Quit saying 'President Trump.' You're spookin' the horses."

"Damn! I forgot to say, 'You're fired.'"

TOP MATTHEW DIFFEE, NOVEMBER 9, 2015 BOTTOM TOM CHENEY, APRIL 19, 2004

*SEE ALSO DOOMSAYERS, TAXES, TWITTER

"Curiouser and curiouser."

TOP ED FISHER, MARCH 25, 1985 BOTTOM PETER KUPER, NOVEMBER 7, 2016

THE NEW YORKER

"It wasn't a lie, Senator, it was a larger truth."

YA KNOW, SLIM, THAT THERE SOVIET MILITARY THREAT IS MIGHTY GROSSLY OVERRATED!

YEP, AND BELIEVE ME, THE FRENCH AIN'T HALF THE LOVERS THEY'RE CRACKED UP TO BE, OL' RUSTY!

AND ANOTHER THING: K.T. TELLS ME RED WINE GOES JES' FINE WITH FISH, THANK YOU!

DEBUNKHOUSE

TOP CHARLES BARSOTTI, APRIL 23, 2007   BOTTOM MICHAEL CRAWFORD, MAY 13, 1991

"I aspired to authenticity, but I never got beyond verisimilitude."

"Say, who the hell's been writing this stuff? It comes perilously close to the truth."

TOP LEE LORENZ, JUNE 25, 2007   BOTTOM BERNARD SCHOENBAUM, DECEMBER 7, 1992

*"Do you swear to tell the truth, the whole truth,
and nothing but the truth, and not in some sneaky relativistic way?"*

TOP GAHAN WILSON, JANUARY 5, 1987

TOP CHARLES BARSOTTI, APRIL 16, 2007   BOTTOM CHARLES BARSOTTI, NOVEMBER 3, 2008

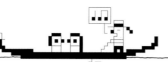

TOP JACK ZIEGLER, SEPTEMBER 28, 1987   BOTTOM SMILBY, JULY 6, 1968

TOP ROZ CHAST, MARCH 31, 2008   BOTTOM MICK STEVENS, MARCH 8, 1993

TOP ROZ CHAST, FEBRUARY 10, 2003   BOTTOM DANNY SHANAHAN, JULY 10, 1995

TOP TOM CHENEY, OCTOBER 22, 2007   BOTTOM LEO CULLUM, JULY 21, 1997

"Well, if we got nothing else, we got great mileage."

"At least he died at home."

TOP ARNIE LEVIN, JUNE 28, 1982   BOTTOM DANNY SHANAHAN, SEPTEMBER 29, 1997

"My doctor told me to take it easy."

TOP BOB MANKOFF, OCTOBER 29, 2007 BOTTOM JACK ZIEGLER, JULY 23, 1979

"Honey, your head's through the armhole again."

"Hold your hat! Here we go!"

TOP MIKE TWOHY, FEBRUARY 5, 2001   BOTTOM DANA FRADON, NOVEMBER 30, 1992

"*This year I thought I'd go with a cowl neck, for a change.*"

"*All right! We know you're in there. Come out with your hands up.*"

TOP FRANK MODELL, APRIL 1, 1991 BOTTOM FRANK MODELL, AUGUST 8, 1994

"You'd know that about me if you followed me on Twitter."

TOP WILLIAM HAEFELI, DECEMBER 13, 2010   BOTTOM FARLEY KATZ, OCTOBER 11, 2010

"Today's service will be using the hashtag '#Jerrysdead.'"

COREY PANDOLPH, OCTOBER 17, 2011

"Demi Moore had a really sad tweet."

"Anyone following me on Twitter already knows what I did this past summer."

TOP BRUCE KAPLAN, OCTOBER 11, 2010   BOTTOM ALEX GREGORY, SEPTEMBER 5, 2011

*SEE ALSO BLUEBIRD OF HAPPINESS, FACEBOOK, TRUMP

*"Says here he leaves behind a wife, two children,
and forty-seven Twitter followers."*

*"hey fans! im at bat,. btm 9th, bases loaded, score
tied—oops, jst got called strike1!"*

TOP MATTHEW DIFFEE, JANUARY 24, 2011   BOTTOM ALEX GREGORY, APRIL 19, 2010

U.F.O.S
ULCERS
UNCLE SAM
UNEMPLOYMENT
UNICORNS
UNITED NATIONS

"Perhaps, Colin, it would be better not to mention any of this."

"Flying saucers seem to have fulfilled a great <u>need</u> for John."

TOP BERNIE WISEMAN, APRIL 28, 1956   BOTTOM STAN HUNT, JUNE 18, 1966

TOP FRANK MODELL, JANUARY 21, 1967   BOTTOM JAMES STEVENSON, MARCH 20, 1978

PROBED

THE U.F.O. IS a great example of news that stays new. During the saucer sightings of the late nineteen-forties, fuzzy photographs actually appeared in newspapers. The United States Air Force devised the term "unidentified flying objects" simply to distinguish them from identified ones (satellites, weather balloons, planes), not to give credence to the idea of visiting space aliens. But the deliberately dry designation took on a silvery glamour of its own. The first time a U.F.O. visited a *New Yorker* cartoon wasn't long after the Roswell incident; drawn by Alan Dunn in 1950, it refers to the mysterious disappearance of a number of New York garbage cans. Almost four decades later, a Roz Chast cartoon reminds us that **we earthlings remain captivated by the prospect of extraterrestrial passersby.** Her "Irrefutable Evidence" of a U.F.O. landing features some adorable pictures of aliens that the witnesses to the incident drew "under hypnosis." If aliens do come for us, let's hope they have a good sense of humor. ♦

ALAN DUNN, MAY 20, 1950

"Why bother to phone? They'll just say it's swamp gas."

ROBERT DAY, APRIL 16, 1966

*SEE ALSO AIR TRAVEL, EXPERIMENTS, SPACE ALIENS

IRREFUTABLE EVIDENCE

fragments of UFO that crash-landed last week near Lambert's Corner, Saskatchewan

Soil taken from site

Some photos taken just prior to landing of craft

Enlarged photo (B.)

Drawings done by Mrs. Kitty Nederson, witness, while under hypnosis

Tape recording of nearby dog barking uncontrollably at time of visitation

R. Chast

"Did you notice that they finally finished the Bruckner Interchange?"

TOP ROZ CHAST, MAY 9, 1988   BOTTOM DONALD REILLY, NOVEMBER 26, 1973

"I'll have the crab Newburg, but don't tell my ulcer."

*"Because of you, my darling, I've never had an ulcer. I've never needed a psychiatrist.
When I poured out my troubles, you listened. When I ranted and raved, you listened.
Thank you, my angel, for listening."*

"Who listened?"

TOP ROBERT WEBER, JANUARY 24, 1977   BOTTOM EDWARD FRASCINO, JUNE 5, 1971

*"I've noticed that the point during a discussion at which you begin to worry about my ulcer
is invariably the point at which I begin to turn the tide."*

"You're giving me <u>ulcers</u>!"

TOP EVERETT OPIE, APRIL 21, 1975   BOTTOM WILLIAM STEIG, OCTOBER 18, 1958

"I ain't got much money, but I ain't got ulcers, either."

"Underneath my gruff exterior lies an ulcer."

TOP WILLIAM STEIG, MAY 20, 1961 BOTTOM CHON DAY, MARCH 29, 1976

"*Bad news—that fire in your belly is an ulcer.*"

"*What gets me is his having ulcers and being a failure.*"

TOP BOB MANKOFF, SEPTEMBER 9, 1991   BOTTOM SYDNEY HOFF, NOVEMBER 17, 1951

"I'm sorry about this, but I'm afraid I just can't wait till April 15th."

"Uncle Sam? Strange sort of name. Are you foreign?"

TOP LEE LORENZ, MARCH 20, 1971 BOTTOM J.B. HANDELSMAN, DECEMBER 9, 1972

*"In view of our equal-opportunity stance, all those in favor
of adding an Aunt Sam to the board say 'Aye.'"*

*"9:30: Pledge allegiance. 10: Wave flag. 10:30: Sing 'Yankee Doodle.'
11: Show true colors. 11:30: Sing 'God Bless America.' 12: Picnic lunch. 1:30: Wave flag…"*

TOP HENRY MARTIN, JUNE 4, 1990   BOTTOM HENRY MARTIN, JULY 2, 1990

"Don't tell me this news isn't being managed."

"Who was it that said, 'Patriotism is the last refuge of a scoundrel'?"

TOP DANA FRADON, JULY 31, 1965   BOTTOM WILLIAM O'BRIAN, JANUARY 31, 1970

"*Get me the Statue of Liberty.*"

"*Hey, this is on me!*"

TOP MISCHA RICHTER, MARCH 31, 1975 MIDDLE MISCHA RICHTER, APRIL 26, 1993 BOTTOM BOB MANKOFF, JUNE 24, 1985

UNEMPLOYMENT
INSURANCE

"Go home, I tell you! The recession is over!"

"I've stopped looking for work, which, I believe, helps the economic numbers."

TOP AL ROSS, AUGUST 25, 1975   BOTTOM LEO CULLUM, JANUARY 26, 2004

*"I may have something rather outside your field.
Would you consider indentured servitude?"*

"On the other hand, my weekends are seven days long."

TOP LEE LORENZ, NOVEMBER 29, 1993   BOTTOM LEO CULLUM, APRIL 20, 2009

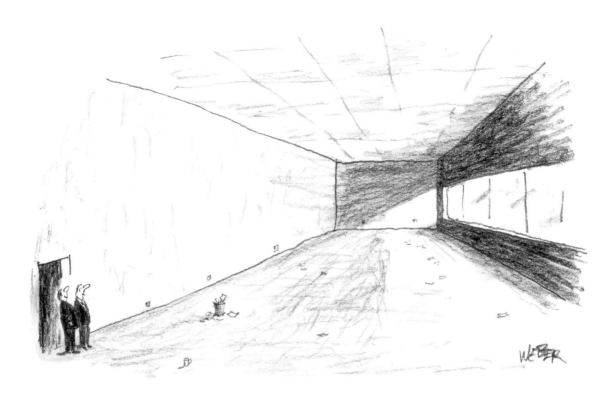

"Well, that does it Charlie—we've outsourced everything."

"I don't like six-percent unemployment, either. But I can live with it."

TOP ROBERT WEBER, JUNE 27, 2005   BOTTOM LEE LORENZ, OCTOBER 28, 1974

*SEE ALSO ARTISTS, ROBOTS, YOU'RE FIRED

"*Take the severance package, Hayward. The rest of the board wanted a ritual slaying.*"

"*We don't fire people here, Thompson, we tag them and release them into the wild.*"

TOP LEO CULLUM, JUNE 5, 2006 BOTTOM GLEN LE LIEVRE, OCTOBER 17, 2005

"It certainly doesn't look like one of your usual unicorns."

TOP FRANK MODELL, OCTOBER 6, 1975   BOTTOM WARREN MILLER, JULY 5, 1969

"Unicorns _do_ exist!"

"I think we need a border fence between Fantasy Land and Sexual-Fantasy Land."

TOP LIANA FINCK, JANUARY 11, 2016   BOTTOM PAUL NOTH, MARCH 31, 2014

*"I used a standard obscure diplomatic code word,
but perhaps it wasn't obscure enough."*

*"What is most depressing is that these platitudes are
being simultaneously translated into five languages."*

TOP ED FISHER, MARCH 20, 1978   BOTTOM KENNETH MAHOOD, JANUARY 23, 1971

"I don't suppose it's terribly important, old chap,
but you're from New Zealand and I'm from the Netherlands."

"Basically, what I have in mind is a twelve-nation conference for the purpose
of setting up a nine-power treaty organization governed by a five-nation steering committee,
which in turn will be dominated by you and me."

TOP J.B. HANDELSMAN, DECEMBER 17, 1966   BOTTOM PETER ARNO, JANUARY 8, 1955

*"If they ever do beat those swords into ploughshares,
they'll end up walloping each other over the head with them."*

STAN HUNT, MAY 23, 1964

"Sh-h-h. It's a birthday card for Liechtenstein.
Sign it and pass it on."

"All I know is when we got here this morning there they were."

TOP DREW DERNAVICH, JUNE 12, 2006   MIDDLE J.B. HANDELSMAN, JULY 15, 1961   BOTTOM DANA FRADON, FEBRUARY 22, 1969

VALENTINES
VAMPIRES
VEGETARIANS
VENDING MACHINES
VERDICTS
VIRGIN *SACRIFICE*
VOLCANOES
VULTURES

"*I didn't send you a valentine.*"

"*I won't need a bag. I'll eat it here.*"

TOP GEORGE BOOTH, FEBRUARY 15, 1988   BOTTOM LEO CULLUM, FEBRUARY 16, 2004

"A pretty rock is always nice at Valentine's Day. Or perhaps another wheel?
Or—gosh—what woman doesn't enjoy a lovely bit of fire?"

"You can't go wrong with the traditional dead mouse."

TOP JACK ZIEGLER, FEBRUARY 12, 2001   BOTTOM AL ROSS, FEBRUARY 17, 1997

HEARTBREAKING

CARTOONISTS ARE HOPELESS romantics—so hopeless, in fact, that they've given up wooing. And Valentine's Day, with its rote rites of devotion—dirt-cheap chocolate, bodega bouquets, Hallmark sonnets—is a holiday custom-made for mockery. Especially with all of those bare-assed cherubs flying everywhere. "Come back, young man. He needs a booster shot," beckons a dissatisfied date to Cupid in Bernard Schoenbaum's depiction of middle-aged *amore.* For humorists, February 14th is the start of hunting season, and it's a target-rich environment. Their archest barbs are drawn at passionless beaus. Look at Mike Twohy's stodgy suitor giving his sweetheart a valentine, with a caveat: "A lot of it is just legal mumbo-jumbo." Bull's-eye. It's not surprising to see satirists giving Eros an eye roll, of course. **Rejection, loneliness, and suppressed emotions are the cartoonists' boon companions, as well as their muses.** True partnership needs no affirmation. Or as George Booth's hubby says glibly to his lifelong mate, "I didn't send you a valentine." And why should he? In comedy, as in camaraderie, it's the thought that counts. ◆

Bernard Schoenbaum

"Come back, young man. He needs a booster shot."

BERNARD SCHOENBAUM, FEBRUARY 11, 2002

"A lot of it is just legal mumbo-jumbo."

TOP JACK ZIEGLER, FEBRUARY 11, 2008   BOTTOM MIKE TWOHY, AUGUST 25, 1997

*SEE ALSO ADVERTISING, DATING, TUNNEL OF LOVE

VALENTINES for ONESELF

TO A GREAT GUY!

I love my biceps,

I love my pecs;

When I look in the mirror,

It's better than sex.

Happy Valentine's day, good buddy!

FROM MY HEART OF HEARTS

TO ME

I was a loser, myopic and fat,

With no social graces at all.

But I've worked on myself
from my socks to my hat,

And now I'm the belle of the ball.

With all my love, darling.

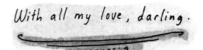

For a Very Special Someone...

I've stuck with me through thick and thin,

No matter what a jerk I've been.

Though opportunities may have beckoned,

I've never left me for even a second.

Eternally yours.

R. Chast

ROZ CHAST, FEBRUARY 13, 1995

"On second thought, I __will__ have the garlic bread."

"This year, Hal, we've decided to concentrate on a few close races, where the undead vote could be decisive."

TOP MICHAEL MASLIN, JANUARY 31, 2011 BOTTOM LEE LORENZ, NOVEMBER 6, 2000

"The guide book says it's the best B.& B. in the Carpathians."

"Wait! First, his attorney."

TOP GAHAN WILSON, JUNE 30, 2003   BOTTOM DANNY SHANAHAN, APRIL 14, 1997

"Tofu in yet another guise?"

"My doctor says you should be drawing more fruits and vegetables."

TOP WARREN MILLER, JUNE 15, 1981   BOTTOM P.C. VEY, JULY 3, 2000

"I can't go much longer without your asking why I'm vegan."

"On second thought, I think I'll have the vegetable plate."

TOP TOM TORO, OCTOBER 17, 2011   BOTTOM MISCHA RICHTER, MARCH 19, 1955

THE BIRTH OF A VEGETARIAN

TOP WARREN MILLER, APRIL 21, 1973 BOTTOM BOB MANKOFF, MAY 25, 1992

"I'll have the vegan."

TOP CHARLES BARSOTTI, JANUARY 22, 2001   BOTTOM MATTHEW DIFFEE, MAY 17, 2010

"Room service here."

TOP TOM CHENEY, AUGUST 24, 2009   BOTTOM LEO CULLUM, MARCH 27, 1978

TOP WILLIAM O'BRIAN, SEPTEMBER 23, 1961 BOTTOM ARNIE LEVIN, NOVEMBER 23, 1992

ARIEL MOLVIG, SEPTEMBER 24, 2012

"And bring a ton of quarters."

TOP FRANK MODELL, JANUARY 19, 1963   BOTTOM TOM CHENEY, DECEMBER 3, 2012

"Your Honor, we find the defendant guilty with a capital 'G'!"

"We find the defendant guilty of being manipulated by the media."

TOP HENRY MARTIN, JUNE 27, 1977   BOTTOM LEE LORENZ, MARCH 18, 1985

"We find the defendant very telegenic."

"We find the defendant guilty on all charges, Your Honor.
On the positive side, we really liked his openness and energy."

TOP MISCHA RICHTER, JULY 12, 1993   BOTTOM MIKE TWOHY, MAY 19, 1997

"We the jury, on the advice of our lawyers, decline to render a verdict."

"We find that all of us, as a society, are to blame,
but only the defendant is guilty."

TOP MIKE TWOHY, AUGUST 3, 1992   BOTTOM MICHAEL MASLIN, FEBRUARY 24, 1997

*SEE ALSO CRIME SCENES, JUDGES, SCARLET LETTER

"Your Honor, we're going to go with the prosecution's spin."

"The bailiff—minus the theatrics—will now read the verdict."

TOP MIKE TWOHY, NOVEMBER 3, 1997   BOTTOM MICHAEL MASLIN, JUNE 4, 2001

"A non-virgin would have had a devastating effect on crop yield."

"We've run out of virgins, O Mighty One!
Will you accept a photographer from 'National Geographic'?"

TOP FRANK COTHAM, DECEMBER 3, 2001   BOTTOM DONALD REILLY, NOVEMBER 20, 1971

"The gods want olive oil, but it has to be virgin olive oil."

"The goddesses want some young dudes."

TOP MICK STEVENS, AUGUST 3, 2009   BOTTOM MICK STEVENS, MAY 11, 2015

"I don't know how the gods feel,
but sacrificing financial advisors makes me feel happy."

"The gods have mixed feelings."

TOP KIM WARP, APRIL 13, 2009 BOTTOM JAMES STEVENSON, JANUARY 5, 1987

"If we accept the unacceptable today, what's the outlook for tomorrow going to be?"

"Several groups have claimed responsibility."

TOP GEORGE BOOTH, JUNE 7, 1993   BOTTOM DANA FRADON, SEPTEMBER 21, 1987

"I now believe in God."

"The gods are antic tonight."

TOP SAM GROSS, JANUARY 22, 1996   BOTTOM DANA FRADON, JUNE 3, 1991

"Whatever the gods are, they aren't angry."

CHARLES ADDAMS, JUNE 13, 1964

"Valerie, I think we should increase our S.P.F."

"Are you <u>sure</u> the gas gauge is working?"

TOP EDWARD FRASCINO, JULY 6, 1998   BOTTOM MISCHA RICHTER, NOVEMBER 15, 1969

"Oh, love handles! We haven't had those in a while."

"Hey, it's my turn to keep the Ray-Bans!"

TOP JULIA SUITS, DECEMBER 25, 2006   BOTTOM DONNA BARSTOW, MARCH 17, 2003

*"The tragedy is I'm a bluebird
locked in the body of a bird of prey."*

"Let's face it. They're all the picture of health!"

TOP ELDON DEDINI, OCTOBER 8, 1973   BOTTOM EVERETT OPIE, AUGUST 29, 1959

*SEE ALSO BLUEBIRD OF HAPPINESS, DEATH, LAWYERS

"It was a good rotting carcass, but it wasn't a great rotting carcass."

"Does anything die and become dessert?"

"Sure, I'd like fresh meat, but it's hard to argue with
carrion's convenience and affordability."

TOP TOM CHENEY, MAY 24, 1999 MIDDLE SAM GROSS, MARCH 15, 2010 BOTTOM ALEX GREGORY, FEBRUARY 2, 2004

SAUL STEINBERG, NOVEMBER 9, 1946

WALL STREET
WAR
WATER COOLER
WEATHER
WEDDING CAKES
WHERE'S WALDO
WHILE YOU WERE OUT
WILLIAM TELL
WINTER
WISE MAN ON MOUNTAIN
WISHING WELL
WITCHES' BROOM
WITCHES' CAULDRON
WOLF IN SHEEP'S CLOTHING
WOODPECKERS
WRESTLING
WRITERS

"I don't expect to do as well as the market. I just want to have a lot of fun."

"Sure, it may be great for us, but it's hell on the markets."

TOP DEAN VIETOR, MARCH 1, 1976 BOTTOM CHRISTOPHER WEYANT, MARCH 6, 2000

MANKOFF

"I'm looking for a hedge against my hedge funds."

"The market was volatile."

TOP BOB MANKOFF, OCTOBER 12, 1998 BOTTOM JAMES STEVENSON, SEPTEMBER 2, 1985

BANK SHOT

O<small>UR NATION'S ENTIRE</small> financial well-being, which is to say each citizen's individual prosperity and happiness, rests on the Dow. Mr. and Mrs. America, that's your pension, your savings, and your mortgage flipping and flopping down there on the trading floor.

To make ordinary citizens believe that this is really all under control, bankers, experts, and commentators bust out the jargon, issuing statements festooned with graphs, numbers, and percentages. But **"the market" remains as murky as ever.** Indeed, just as a loving mother at bedtime will provide a worried child with the smallest details of an imaginary guardian angel's wings, they include heaps of decimal points, as though precision somehow proves that their statistics actually mean something. All these statements, with and without numbers, can be translated roughly as "I have absolutely *no* idea why this is happening." Followed by a dry, avuncular grin. And a gag. ♦

"*Liverwurst is down an eighth, egg-salad is up two and a half,
and peanut-butter-and-jelly remains unchanged.*"

JACK ZIEGLER, JANUARY 7, 1980

*"And, finally, after a day of record trading on Wall Street,
the entire world was owned by Mickey Mouse."*

*"I'll tell you why we were put on this planet.
We were put on this planet to outperform the market!"*

TOP LEE LORENZ, JANUARY 11, 1993 BOTTOM WILLIAM HAMILTON, MARCH 28, 1977

"It's designed to generate electricity by moving with fluctuations in the Dow."

"Dow Jonesy enough for you?"

TOP TOM CHENEY, JULY 4, 2005 BOTTOM JACK ZIEGLER, AUGUST 17, 1998

"I just got a great idea for a war!"

"It's so-so."

TOP MICK STEVENS, JULY 7, 2003 BOTTOM JACK ZIEGLER, OCTOBER 10, 1988

"*My people will get back to your people.*"

"*I do want a war, but I'd like to be asked nicely.*"

TOP ELDON DEDINI, JANUARY 14, 1991 BOTTOM J.B. HANDELSMAN, SEPTEMBER 30, 2002

"World War III? Hmm. O.K., but, remember, nobody gets hurt."

ROBERT WEBER, MARCH 8, 1999

*SEE ALSO MILITARY MEDALS, NAPOLEON, PEACE

"Son, everyone went to college in the sixties—there was a war going on."

"Well, I'm an optimist—I still think peace can be avoided."

TOP BARBARA SMALLER, OCTOBER 11, 1999 BOTTOM BOB MANKOFF, OCTOBER 4, 2010

"Got him last week—he rounds up the strays at the water cooler."

"When you're nailing the numbers, they don't ask questions."

TOP TOM CHENEY, MARCH 8, 2004 BOTTOM C. COVERT DARBYSHIRE, OCTOBER 2, 2006

*"When you're through with that,
there's a water cooler on seven that needs emptying."*

"You always get the good gossip out here around the vodka cooler."

TOP P.C. VEY, FEBRUARY 6, 2006 BOTTOM MATTHEW DIFFEE, JANUARY 12, 2004

"I just thought we should talk more."

MANAGER

TOP DREW DERNAVICH, MAY 19, 2008 MIDDLE BERNIE WISEMAN, NOVEMBER 19, 1955 BOTTOM OTTO SOGLOW, JANUARY 7, 1956

CHARLES ADDAMS, MAY 12, 1973

"I've learned to express my anger through my writing instead."

TOP DREW DERNAVICH, AUGUST 11, 2008 BOTTOM JACK ZIEGLER, SEPTEMBER 29, 2003

"We're expecting some major accumulation."

"Isn't it about time to switch from your
warm-weather chair to your cold-weather chair?"

TOP DAVID SIPRESS, MARCH 14, 2005   BOTTOM P.C. VEY, OCTOBER 9, 2006

CORPORATE SPONSORSHIP COMES TO
HURRICANES

THE VERIZON WIRELESS HURRICANE KANDEE®

THE ~~AOL~~ TIME WARNER HURRICANE LAMAR®

THE BRISTOL-MYERS SQUIBB HURRICANE MIDGE®

MICHAEL CRAWFORD, SEPTEMBER 29. 2003

*"They complain that it's the hottest summer in a hundred years,
but I say, No problem-o."*

"Coggins, get me somebody in weather."

TOP JACK ZIEGLER, JULY 25, 2011   BOTTOM MICK STEVENS, APRIL 28, 2008

TOP FRANK MODELL, OCTOBER 3, 1994 BOTTOM JACK ZIEGLER, JUNE 24, 1985

TOP PETER STEINER, JULY 9, 1979 BOTTOM EVERETT OPIE, JUNE 22, 1987

"Forget it, Carl."

TOP JACK ZIEGLER, APRIL 25, 1994 BOTTOM BILL WOODMAN, FEBRUARY 22, 1988

"Got any plans for later?"

TOP FRANK MODELL, JUNE 1, 1992 BOTTOM MICHAEL CRAWFORD, JANUARY 7, 2002

"Where's Waldo in five years?"

WAITING FOR WALDOT

TOP JASON ADAM KATZENSTEIN, JULY 20, 2015 BOTTOM LIAM WALSH, OCTOBER 17, 2016

KAAMRAN HAFEEZ, FEBRUARY 27, 2012

"While you were out, somebody with three names called."

"While you were out, there was a rift in the space-time continuum."

TOP ARNIE LEVIN, SEPTEMBER 23, 1996 BOTTOM DAVID SIPRESS, JANUARY 13, 2003

*"While you were out, Mr. Sundberg,
the little hand went from the one to the three."*

"While you were out."

TOP BOB MANKOFF, FEBRUARY 3, 1986 BOTTOM TOM CHENEY, NOVEMBER 12, 2001

"While you were out."

TOP MICK STEVENS, APRIL 1, 2002 BOTTOM DANNY SHANAHAN, AUGUST 5, 1991

WHILE YOU WERE OUT*

*"Mr. Weston, while you were out I found your secret
cache of M&M's and polished them off."*

*"Sir, while you were out the baby-doll dress came into fashion,
went out of fashion, and came back with a vengeance."*

TOP HENRY MARTIN, JUNE 1, 1987 BOTTOM BOB MANKOFF, NOVEMBER 7, 1994

Shanahan

TOP DANNY SHANAHAN, SEPTEMBER 15, 2003   BOTTOM ROBERT WEBER, OCTOBER 12, 1968

"Go right in—he's expecting you."

TOP RICHARD McCALLISTER, OCTOBER 8, 1979 BOTTOM MICHAEL MASLIN, FEBRUARY 7, 2005

"Wait, Son. I've got a better idea."

"They're not going to like this in Switzerland."

TOP ROBERT KRAUS, AUGUST 5, 1961 BOTTOM ED FISHER, FEBRUARY 1, 1958

TOP ARNIE LEVIN, FEBRUARY 17, 1975 BOTTOM WARREN MILLER, JUNE 11, 1990

"I'm not wearing any thermal underwear."

TOP TOM TORO AND BENJAMIN SCHWARTZ, FEBRUARY 20, 2014 BOTTOM BOB ECKSTEIN, DECEMBER 9, 2013

"Miss Eisenhart, considering the weather,
I've decided to take the afternoon and February off."

"Don't overdo it, Ira. This isn't even our car."

TOP HENRY MARTIN, FEBRUARY 2, 1987 BOTTOM MICHAEL CRAWFORD, FEBRUARY 12, 2001

"Still snowing upstate?"

"Think spring."

TOP GAHAN WILSON, MARCH 14, 1988   BOTTOM FRANK MODELL, JANUARY 18, 1988

"No two flakes are alike. It almost makes you want to believe in something."

TOP WARREN MILLER, DECEMBER 30, 1985   BOTTOM FELIPE GALINDO, MARCH 1, 2010

"*The first step toward enlightenment is dissillusionment.*"

"*I'm on sabbatical.*"

TOP MIKE TWOHY, FEBRUARY 11, 2008 BOTTOM DREW DERNAVICH, APRIL 16, 2007

"*No, but I can tell you the meaning of whole or term life insurance.*"

"*Mom?*"

TOP MICHAEL SHAW, JUNE 9, 1997   BOTTOM HARRY BLISS, OCTOBER 18, 2010

UPWARD MOBILITY

CARTOONS ABOUT WISE MEN on mountains generally impart more humor than wisdom. The climbers crave enlightenment, but the air is thin up there. And why has the sage chosen such an inconvenient location? Exhaustive analysis reveals that the sage isn't on the mountaintop because he's wise; he has become wise by dwelling on the mountaintop. Having separated himself from the turmoil of humanity and spent years alone with his thoughts, he can tell you that you shouldn't desire what you desire. Including the wisdom he has to dispense. Speaking of wisdom: why does it have to be a wise *guy*? Harry Bliss's cartoon from 2010 shows a climber seeing his mother at the summit. He could have saved himself a long journey if he'd listened to her from the start. ♦

"I hope you like sports metaphors."

JOE DATOR, MAY 18, 2009

"No, I don't have any weed."

"I'm not a guru. I'm just hanging out here till my renovation is done."

TOP ERIC LEWIS, OCTOBER 15, 2001 BOTTOM ROBERT LEIGHTON, AUGUST 13, 2007

"I wish to be cannier."

"From Ottawa! Now, how about that!
I must have tossed in a Canadian dime!"

TOP WARREN MILLER, AUGUST 19, 1972   BOTTOM CLAUDE SMITH, SEPTEMBER 16, 1972

"It can't be much good."

TOP DANA FRADON, MAY 8, 1971 BOTTOM DANA FRADON, JULY 3, 1971

"Hey! Congratulations, Mister! Yours was the one-millionth wish!"

"I wish I were rich, handsome, well tailored and well groomed, gracious, elegant, dashing, distinguished, and yet much admired by my peers."

TOP HENRY MARTIN, AUGUST 31, 1968 BOTTOM HENRY MARTIN, APRIL 3, 1971

*SEE ALSO PRAYERS, RAINBOWS, VENDING MACHINES

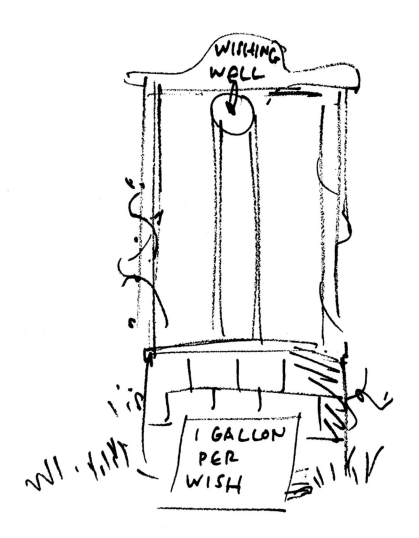

TOP CHARLES ADDAMS, FEBRUARY 24, 1968 BOTTOM JAMES STEVENSON, FEBRUARY 4, 1974

"Look! No broom!"

TOP JAMES STEVENSON, NOVEMBER 4, 1985 BOTTOM ROBERT KRAUS, OCTOBER 31, 1964

TOP LEE LORENZ, NOVEMBER 2, 1981 BOTTOM FRANK MODELL , OCTOBER 27, 1962

"She's a classic."

"I just got tired of the same old hat."

TOP EDWARD KOREN, OCTOBER 30, 1989 BOTTOM CHARLES ADDAMS, NOVEMBER 3, 1980

"It seems to get worse every Halloween."

ED FISHER, NOVEMBER 1, 1969

"I love the profession, but after all these years I'm still basically not a night person."

"Call me sentimental, but I always add a few cherries on Washington's Birthday."

TOP DONALD REILLY, SEPTEMBER 28, 1981   BOTTOM EDWARD FRASCINO, FEBRUARY 21, 1977

"*Is that all it says about eye of newt—add to taste?*"

"*Does this poison smell weird to you?*"

TOP FRANK MODELL, APRIL 18, 1983 BOTTOM ALEX GREGORY, OCTOBER 26, 2009

CHARLES ADDAMS, OCTOBER 29, 1984

"I've thrown in some prescription drugs that don't interact well."

"Oh, no, my dear! Add buffering, you still only get one analgesic."

TOP FRANK COTHAM, OCTOBER 28, 2002 BOTTOM JAMES STEVENSON, JULY 18, 1959

"What I really hate is knowing that I'm doing this exactly the way my mother did it."

TOP ROZ CHAST, OCTOBER 25, 2010   BOTTOM DONALD REILLY, NOVEMBER 3, 1997

"Too sweet. Use less revenge."

"Mom, can I have the broom tonight?"

TOP EDWARD FRASCINO, FEBRUARY 27, 1978 BOTTOM CHARLES ADDAMS, AUGUST 21, 1954

"Sometimes I worry I'm a wolf dressed as me."

TOP FRANK MODELL, OCTOBER 19, 1981   BOTTOM BRUCE KAPLAN, FEBRUARY 2, 2004

"Now <u>there's</u> a complicated wolf."

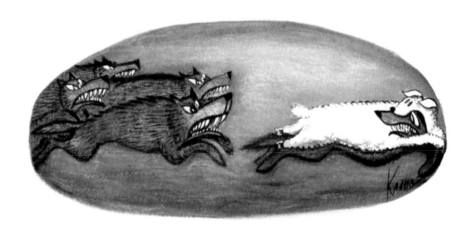

"Fellows, it's <u>me!</u>"

TOP PETER ARNO, APRIL 13, 1957 BOTTOM ROBERT KRAUS, APRIL 11, 1964

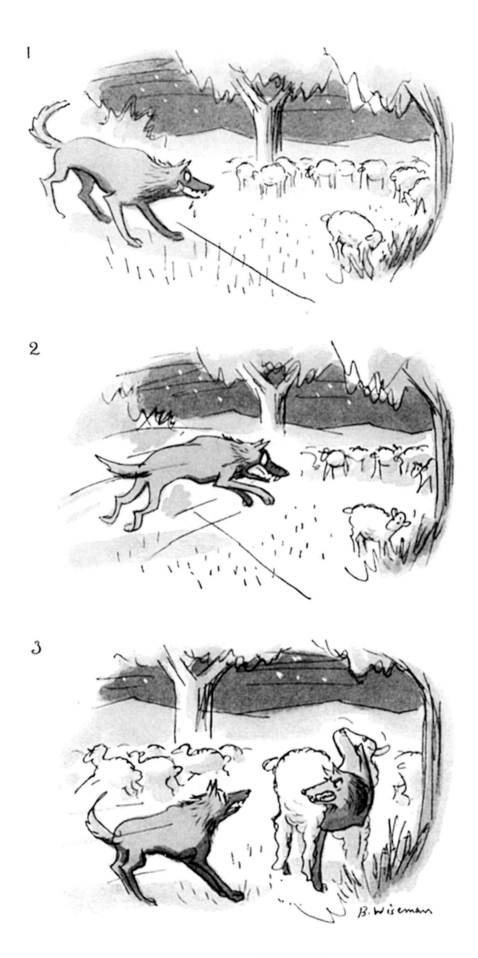

BERNIE WISEMAN, AUGUST 30, 1952

*SEE ALSO CAT VS. MOUSE, HORSE COSTUME, POLITICIANS

"*That's a marvelous disguise! I almost ate you.*"

"*It's not a sexual thing—I just enjoy dressing up in sheep's clothing.*"

TOP SAM GROSS, NOVEMBER 14, 2011 BOTTOM DAVID SIPRESS, JUNE 6, 2016

"Look, Buster, I'm trying to get some shut-eye."

TOP MORT GERBERG, JANUARY 23, 2012   BOTTOM FRANK MODELL, JUNE 25, 1960

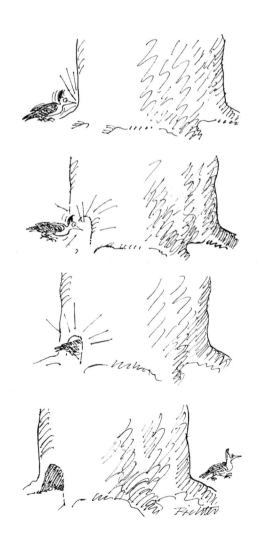

TOP FRANK MODELL, JUNE 25, 1960 BOTTOM MISCHA RICHTER, JUNE 22, 1981

"Ignore them."

"And in this corner, wearing blue trunks and representing the middle class…"

TOP CHARLES BARSOTTI, JUNE 10, 1991   BOTTOM ED FISHER, JANUARY 10, 1977

"It's hard to believe these things aren't prearranged."

"You know the rules—no hitting with the closed fist, no biting, no eye-gouging.
And I want you to remember at all times that you are being televised and are expected to
set an example of clean sportsmanship to young American womanhood…"

TOP MISCHA RICHTER, MARCH 8, 1947 BOTTOM ELDON DEDINI, JULY 28, 1951

1.

2.

ALAIN, AUGUST 16, 1947

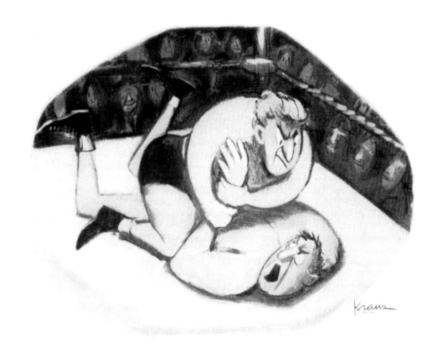

"What goes on? You trying to win?"

TOP ROZ CHAST, FEBRUARY 11, 2002 BOTTOM ROBERT KRAUS, MAY 28, 1955

"Finish it? Why would I want to finish it?"

"I want to write what I know, but all I know is writing workshops."

TOP W.B. PARK, JULY 29, 1985   BOTTOM BARBARA SMALLER, NOVEMBER 19, 2001

WRITER'S FOOD PYRAMID

PIZZA

THE ALCOHOLS

THE NICOTINES

THE CAFFEINES

"Write about dogs!"

TOP TOM CHENEY, JUNE 16, 2003 BOTTOM GEORGE BOOTH, APRIL 5, 1976

JAMES JOYCE'S REFRIGERATOR

DAVID JACOBSON, SEPTEMBER 25, 1989

"We're still pretty far apart. I'm looking for a six-figure advance and they're refusing to read the manuscript."

"I wrote another five hundred words. Can I have another cookie?"

TOP BOB MANKOFF, MARCH 30, 1987 BOTTOM MICK STEVENS, DECEMBER 24, 2001

"*This is definitely the last time for Chapter Seventeen!*"

"*Yep, that's it—seven pages. I only write what I know.*"

TOP GEORGE BOOTH, APRIL 13, 1992   BOTTOM ROBERT WEBER, OCTOBER 4, 1999

*SEE ALSO EDGAR ALLEN POE, LIGHT BULB IDEAS, MEET THE AUTHOR

"Wait a minute. Where am I going? I'm a writer."

TOP CHARLES BARSOTTI, JUNE 27, 1994 BOTTOM LEO CULLUM, JUNE 27, 1994

X-RATED
X-RAYS
XEROX
YACHTS
YALE
YOGA
YOU'RE FIRED
YUPPIES
ZEBRAS
ZEN
ZEUS
ZOMBIES
ZOOS
ZORRO

"*Live and learn, Clarabelle.*"

"*I swear I wasn't looking at smut—I was just stealing music.*"

TOP BARNEY TOBEY, MARCH 27, 1971   BOTTOM ALEX GREGORY, FEBRUARY 4, 2002

"It's out of stock right now, but we have something just as dirty."

"My parents are so busy checking the computer
that they never think of this."

TOP CHON DAY, OCTOBER 19, 1946   BOTTOM PAT BYRNES, AUGUST 31, 2009

X
Y
Z

"Is there any chance it will be held over?
I won't be seventeen until next Tuesday."

"What? I filed our taxes online and now I'm celebrating."

TOP CHARLES MARTIN, OCTOBER 3, 1970   BOTTOM WILLIAM HAEFELI, APRIL 16, 2007

"What happened to 'Erotica'?"

"And just what was that little window you clicked off when I came in?"

TOP SAM GROSS, AUGUST 25, 1997   BOTTOM ARNIE LEVIN, SEPTEMBER 27, 1999

X
Y
Z

"He appears to have eaten some homework."

TOP JOSEPH FARRIS, NOVEMBER 4, 1967   BOTTOM ARNIE LEVIN, MAY 26, 1997

*"Dr. Horton and I have discovered something we don't like.
Our hope is that you, on the other hand, will grow to like it."*

TOP RICHARD DECKER, JANUARY 17, 1948   BOTTOM LARRY HAT, APRIL 23, 2001

X
Y
Z

PICTURE
OF HEALTH

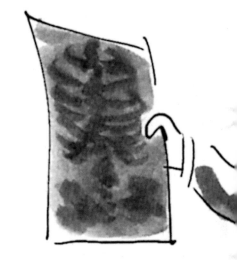

A GOOD CARTOON can succinctly state a truth about human nature that lies deep inside of us. A good cartoon about X-rays can succinctly make a joke about what's actually inside of us. What many X-ray cartoons also reveal is a slight suspicion of medicine—and perhaps a note about bedside manner. What if doctors were uncaring goofs? They'd likely be run out of their practice, and run into a cartoon in *The New Yorker.*

Comedy often arises from the contrast between what we are and what we pretend to be, but it can also arise from the snappy reduction—the sense of a complicated problem that turns out to have a surprisingly simple solution. **It can be awkward when our insides are outed.** But physicians, too, have internal concerns. In Richard Decker's 1948 cartoon, a doctor uses a mirror to check out his own rib cage: an in-depth selfie. Discouraging, but maybe we shouldn't judge too harshly—after all, it's what's on the inside that counts. ♦

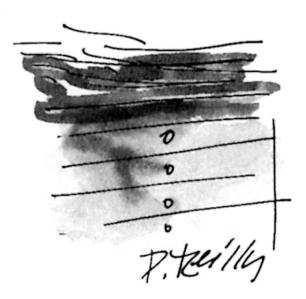

"Basically, there's nothing wrong with you that what's right with you can't cure."

DONALD REILLY, FEBRUARY 8, 1993

X
Y
Z

*"Miss Caldwell, write twenty letters, make five Xerox copies of each,
feed the whole lot into the shredder, and then, if it's five o'clock, you may go home."*

"Well, don't just sit there. Xerox something."

TOP J.B. HANDELSMAN, JULY 31, 1978   BOTTOM HENRY MARTIN, MARCH 9, 1968

*"Xerox Corporation. How do you do and how do you do
and how do you do again?"*

"Waiter, please have this napkin Xeroxed and notarized."

TOP HENRY MARTIN, APRIL 13, 1968   BOTTOM DONALD REILLY, JANUARY 16, 1984

"*Landlubber!*"

"*What is it, Ira, that draws man inexorably back to the sea?*"

TOP MISCHA RICHTER, AUGUST 21, 1971 BOTTOM LEE LORENZ, AUGUST 9, 2004

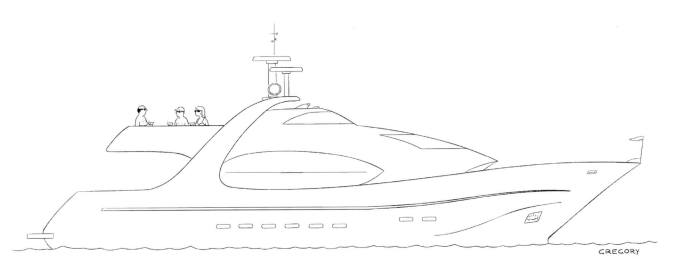

"*It's a little present I gave myself for being so rich.*"

"*Everybody comfortable? Got what they want? Know their place?*"

TOP ALEX GREGORY, SEPTEMBER 3, 2001   BOTTOM WILLIAM HAMILTON, AUGUST 23, 1993

X
Y
Z

"Gosh, Ethel, all I know is he had a ready wit at Yale."

"I think it's unquestionably the finest letter you've ever written to the 'Yale Alumni Magazine.'"

TOP STAN HUNT, MAY 18, 1987   BOTTOM JAMES STEVENSON, FEBRUARY 22, 1969

*"Oh, yes, Harold is doing very well at Yale.
He's been tapped for Skin and Bones."*

TOP HELEN HOKINSON, MAY 12, 1934   BOTTOM HARRY BLISS, NOVEMBER 27, 2006

"Well, if it's true we're the last two people on earth,
it's comforting to know you're a Yale man."

ELDON DEDINI, AUGUST 15, 1959

*SEE ALSO EDUCATION, GRADUATION, YUPPIES

MISCHA RICHTER, JULY 10, 1954

"When did everybody stop jogging?"

TOP DAVID SIPRESS, MAY 20, 2002   BOTTOM SAM GROSS, SEPTEMBER 23, 2002

"You do yoga like a guy."

"Boy, I'm going to pay for this tomorrow at yoga class."

TOP ERIC LEWIS, AUGUST 12, 2002   BOTTOM ALEX GREGORY, APRIL 19, 2004

ALL TWISTED

As with the grateful dead, the problem with yoga isn't so much yoga itself as the people who devote themselves to it. What began, innocently enough, as a spiritual and physical exercise in India millennia ago has exploded into a billion-dollar industry bent on making your butt look good in hundred-dollar workout pants. For cartoonists, who are as keen-eyed for hypocrisy as a crow is for tinfoil, there's a lot to seize on here, not least because people who are super into yoga are just *so goddamn serious* about the fact that they're into yoga. It's just one of an array of social signifiers of a Certain Type: **the Crunchy Urbanite, the Rich Hippie, the kind of person who brews her own kombucha,** eschews sugar and white flour, and posts a lot of stuff on Facebook about "toxins."

Of course, by now yoga has become so mainstream that it has lost a bit of its non-violent punch as a target for ridicule—even your average, non-kombucha-making Joe and Jane are likely to have taken a class or two at their local Y. The cartoonist's gimlet eye has turned more toward folks who use words like "artisanal" and name their kids after species of trees. But still: say "namaste" to a cartoonist and see if she doesn't jot down a retort that's graphic in more ways than one. ◆

MISCHA RICHTER, JULY 26, 1993

X
Y
Z

"Special assignment, Chaswick. I need you to test our severance package."

"I've finally learned not to measure my worth by
how many employees I have."

TOP JOHN CALDWELL, MAY 10, 1999   BOTTOM FRANK COTHAM, MAY 25, 2009

"Do you have any problem being fired by a woman?"

"Sit down, Brad—I've got some character-building news for you."

TOP PETER STEINER, JUNE 3, 2002   BOTTOM BOB MANKOFF, DECEMBER 18, 2000

"Bad news, Gilchrist—somehow you've come to someone's attention."

"We'd like you to take early retirement,
retroactive to the day you started working here."

TOP CHARLES BARSOTTI, MARCH 4, 2002 BOTTOM P.C. VEY, APRIL 9, 2001

*SEE ALSO JOB INTERVIEWS, TRUMP, UNEMPLOYMENT

"Boy, did I tell off my boss this morning—my ex-boss, that is."

"I'm not going to lie to you, Saunders—I'm going to lie to you."

TOP JOSEPH MIRACHI, JULY 27, 1968 BOTTOM ALEX GREGORY, AUGUST 31, 2009

X
Y
Z

"As mountains go, this one is fairly yuppie."

Yuppitniks

TOP JAMES STEVENSON, FEBRUARY 12, 1990   BOTTOM WARREN MILLER, APRIL 15, 1985

"We hate to shop."

YUPPIE STREET GANGS

TOP EDWARD KOREN, OCTOBER 14, 1985   BOTTOM JACK ZIEGLER, AUGUST 25, 1986

X
Y
Z

"Why is it that they always go around talking about
how they earned their stripes?"

"Oh, there you are!"

TOP ED FISHER, NOVEMBER 29, 1999   BOTTOM SYDNEY HOFF, MAY 21, 1960

"Bummer."

"Looking at us objectively, I'd say we were really quite stunning creatures."

TOP STEVE DUENES, NOVEMBER 17, 2003   BOTTOM BARNEY TOBEY, OCTOBER 23, 1965

*"Right. How could anyone look at a rotting zebra corpse
and not believe there's a God?"*

"Oh, yes, sir, the zebra is fresh."

TOP CHARLES BARSOTTI, JANUARY 10, 2000   BOTTOM CHARLES BARSOTTI, OCTOBER 15, 2001

MISCHA RICHTER, MAY 20, 1985

X
Y
Z

"I'm sorry, but Mr. Wallace is One with the All right now.
Would you care to leave a message?"

TOP WARREN MILLER, FEBRUARY 19, 1966   BOTTOM STAN HUNT, MAY 2, 1964

*"To be may be reason enough for you to be,
but to be isn't reason enough for me to be."*

*"You can tell us the sound of one hand clapping here,
or you can tell us downtown."*

TOP JAMES MULLIGAN, JANUARY 1, 1966   BOTTOM PAUL NOTH, APRIL 27, 2009

X
Y
Z

"I've been saving this baby for the stock market."

DONALD REILLY, MARCH 31, 1997

"Looks like you're out for the season—you've got a torn rotator cuff."

"If you're so good, why can't you ever strike twice in the same place?"

TOP BOB MANKOFF, APRIL 18, 1994 BOTTOM MISCHA RICHTER, SEPTEMBER 23, 1967

"No, no, that won't be necessary—they're doing a pretty good job on themselves."

"I used to do it all myself, but now I have my lawyers handle it."

TOP FARLEY KATZ, DECEMBER 15, 2008   BOTTOM MICK STEVENS, MAY 24, 1999

"Hi, I'm Zeus, the man behind the myth."

"And now here's Zeus with the weather."

TOP PETER STEINER, JANUARY 29, 2001   BOTTOM SAM GROSS, JULY 2, 1990

*"You know, if we didn't walk this way
we might get close enough to eat someone."*

"Yeah, they're slow, but we're saving a bundle on health care."

TOP DAVID BORCHART, JUNE 20, 2016   BOTTOM LEE LORENZ, MARCH 14, 2011

NIGHT OF THE LIVING WILL

The zombies were halfway across the living room when
they noticed that "Friends" was on.

TOP JOHN O'BRIEN, FEBRUARY 18, 1991   BOTTOM GLEN LE LIEVRE, APRIL 19, 2004

STAGGERING GENIUS

THE LATE GEORGE Romero explained his zombiephilia thus: "You can't really get angry at them, they have no hidden agendas, they are what they are. I sympathize with them." When you get beyond the blackened eye sockets, drool, and raging appetite for human meat, the common zombie is, after all, our brother. O.K., maybe young zombies don't have super-high S.A.T. scores, but that's just how it works out for the undead teen! When all you can think about is the ripe, warm taste of mortally wounded flesh on your tongue, you just don't have time to develop a strong foundation in general knowledge.

At least these people know what they want. And, unlike so many guilt-ridden, over-psychologized creatures of the twenty-first century, they're not ashamed of admitting it. The zombie gag, then, often centers on **the single-mindedness of this subspecies.** There are no liberal or conservative zombies. They often travel in packs. They have their own lurching way of walking. And their cultural cohesiveness is demonstrated by the fact that they even have their own holiday anthem, "All I Want for Christmas Is You!" If we were the teensiest bit more honest, if we could just be who we are, wouldn't each of us see the zombie in the mirror? ◆

ROZ CHAST, APRIL 7, 2003

"One senior and one undead."

TOP DAVID SIPRESS, JANUARY 30, 2012 BOTTOM BENJAMIN SCHWARTZ, MAY 12, 2014

*SEE ALSO ELVIS, INSOMNIA, TOMBSTONES

"I contemplate Zombie number seventeen."

TOP JACK ZIEGLER, MARCH 5, 2001   BOTTOM ROZ CHAST, OCTOBER 18, 2010

"Lots of new faces this year."

*"'Born in conservation,' if you don't mind.
'Captivity' has negative connotations."*

TOP GEORGE PRICE, MARCH 31, 1980   BOTTOM J.B. HANDELSMAN, MARCH 22, 1993

*"We had to let the animals go.
No one informed them of their rights when they were arrested."*

"So near and yet so far!"

TOP J.B. HANDELSMAN, AUGUST 5, 1996   BOTTOM GAHAN WILSON, JANUARY 30, 2012

"They expect so much and we have so little to give!"

*"With the budget cuts and then the personnel layoffs,
we've had to ask everyone to pitch in."*

TOP JAMES STEVENSON, SEPTEMBER 23, 1961   BOTTOM LEE LORENZ, MAY 3, 1976

*"He didn't do anything, Gregory.
This is a zoo."*

"Yes, I see the elephant!"

"He has a sunny disposition, hasn't he?"

TOP DAVID SIPRESS, APRIL 15, 2002   MIDDLE SYDNEY HOFF, JANUARY 27, 1962   BOTTOM CHON DAY, APRIL 2, 1966

XYZ

TOP ROZ CHAST, NOVEMBER 29, 2010   BOTTOM J.P. RINI, JULY 20, 1998

"I suppose, Muriel, that, in my own curious way,
I've always loved you."

THE MARKS OF ZORRO

TOP LEO CULLUM, JULY 31, 1978 BOTTOM DANNY SHANAHAN, NOVEMBER 19, 1990

X
Y
Z